Gospels, Series A

Augsburg
Sermons for
Children

Augsburg

MINNEAPOLIS

AUGSBURG SERMONS FOR CHILDREN
Gospels, Series A

Interior design: Virginia Aretz, Northwestern Printcrafters
Cover design: Lecy Design

Library of Congress Cataloging-in-Publication Data

Augsburg sermons for children : Gospels, series A
    p. cm.
  ISBN 0-8066-2621-6 (alk. paper)
    1. Bible. N.T. Gospels—Children's sermons.   2. Lutheran Church—
Sermons.   3. Church year sermons.   4. Sermons, American.
I. Augsburg Fortress (Publisher)
BS2555.4.A945   1992
252'.53—dc20   92-27959
                                                                      CIP

The paper used in this publication meets the minimum requirements of American National Standard for Information Sciences—Permanence of Paper for Printed Library Materials, ANSI Z329.48-1984. ∞™

Manufactured in the U.S.A.   AF 9–2621

96   4   5   6   7   8   9   10

Contents

The Rev. Eldon Weisheit
Fountain of Life Lutheran Church
Tucson, Arizona

The Rev. Lisa Stafford
St. Peter Lutheran Church
Trenton, Ohio

Gail Wettstein
Staff Attorney, Oklahoma Court of Criminal Appeals
Oklahoma City, Oklahoma

The Rev. C. Michael Cunningham

Preface

—————— • ——————

When the disciples of Jesus tried to prevent parents from bringing their children to him, Jesus stopped the disciples and told them to let the children come to him; he included children in his ministry.

Sometimes the church has done little to include children in its worship services. Now many pastors and church leaders are exploring a number of ways for children to participate, and the children's sermon has great potential.[1] During this special time, the gospel can be communicated to children in ways particularly appropriate for them, taking seriously children's concerns, level of understanding, and interests. Children are full members in the household of faith, and nothing is more important than sowing the seeds of the gospel early in life.

The goal of this book is to present children's sermons through which children can begin to realize the immensity of God's love for them and God's acceptance of them as they are. Even though the messages and activities use simple language and basic concepts, the gospel is not trivialized. The writers of these children's sermons hope that the children will experience God's love and feel the joy that such good news brings.

The introductory material for each sermon provides helpful information for those using this book. After the Sunday and Gospel text, there are three headings: Focus, Experience, and Preparation. The focus statement encapsulates the theme, the experience statement tells what activity is planned, and the preparations statement describes what needs to be done ahead of time. Though adaptations can be made, these keys for effective use provide basic information about the authors' intentions.

Because "doing" is as important as "talking" with children, the children's sermons in this book are designed to encourage active participation as well as conversation with the children. The emphasis is on all levels of being: not just what to think about (the intel-

---

1. *Including Children in Worship* by Elizabeth J. Sandell is an excellent resource that gives many practical ideas beyond children's sermons (Augsburg, Minneapolis).

lectual) but also their feelings about relationships, experiences, and discoveries (the affective).

Some of the children's sermons begin with the use of props, objects, or special arrangements, but these sermons are not like some object lessons that ask children to make symbolic connections between an object and a spiritual concept. Such abstract thinking is beyond most children's ability. Objects and props in these sermons are from the children's own experiences and the concepts are on a level they can understand.

As you plan to present these children's sermons, you will bring your own style and gifts to your time with the children. Your gifts of spontaneity, flexibility, and creativity will give life to the messages. Children are usually eager to join in the experiences you lead, and your enthusiasm will help them gain much from your time together.

Your primary audience will be the children who come forward to participate, but other children too hesitant or shy to come up, as well as adults and youth, will also be listening and watching. When you ask the children questions, everyone in the congregation will be listening and probably answering to themselves.

The congregation may respond to the dialogue that is part of the children's sermon with warm, affirming laughter. This is usually not disruptive but rather extends the dialogue and lets you know the congregation is listening. There can be a temptation to play to this larger audience, but do not give in to it. The children will sense that they are no longer your primary focus, and you will break the essential bond you have been developing with them.

Effective dialogue develops with good questions and responses. Open questions, such as "What do you do when you know a storm is coming?", generate interesting responses. Because you do not suggest a particular answer, you are more likely to get authentic and sometimes unexpected responses. Closed questions, ones that can be answered with yes or no or a brief, factual answer rarely lead to further conversation. Yet some closed questions are helpful to define words or identify a person or action. For example, "What was Jesus doing when the storm came up?" (Luke 8:22-25) can be answered, "He was sleeping." Following that with open questions will involve the children more fully.

If an object or a prop is part of a children's sermon, let the children hold it and handle it when that is possible. They will learn more from their own experience than from simply watching you.

Asking a couple of children to help you open the backpack or hold
the posterboard helps them feel needed and important.

Children's sermons that are more grace oriented than law oriented convey God's love more clearly. As much as possible, messages to children should communicate how God shows grace
through Jesus Christ; how God has worked through the lives of
people in Bible times, throughout the ages, and today; and how
God loves each one of them very much.[2]

---

2. Special thanks to Lisa Stafford and Gail Wettstein who provided some of the material used in this preface.

First Sunday in Advent

———————————————— • ————————————————

The Gospel: Matthew 24:37-44

Focus: Advent is a special time to think about Jesus.

Experience: The children will talk about forgetting, and especially forgetting about Jesus. They will be introduced to the Advent wreath as a way to remember Jesus.

Preparation: Before the service, tie a string around one of your fingers. This sermon centers around an Advent wreath. If your church does not have one, bring one that the children can see. Have the children gather around the Advent wreath. If it has not already been lit, have a match or something else ready to light the first Advent candle. Otherwise, simply point to the lighted candle.

Let's Remember

Have you ever forgotten to do something that you were supposed to do? I know when I was growing up, my job was to take out the garbage. Sometimes I'd forget to do that. The garbage would start to pile up. But my mom would remind me or I'd see the full garbage pail and then I'd remember what I was supposed to do.

Have you ever forgotten to do something? (*Talk with the children about this. Engage the children in a discussion about things they have forgotten. You might be prepared for answers like, "picking up my room," or "doing my homework."*)

We all forget things sometimes. Do you know what I do, to help me remember things? Sometimes I tie a string around my finger. (*Show the children the string around your finger.*) That reminds me that I have something to do. What do you do when you need to remember something? (*Expect responses such as "write a note," or "circle a date."*) It helps us to remember if we see something that reminds us.

Sometimes we can even forget about Jesus. That's sad, because Jesus is our Lord and our friend. But sometimes we get too busy with other things, or we turn our attention elsewhere. We just kind of forget about Jesus.

Does that sometimes happen to you? (*If the children do not agree, don't force them to. Simply continue.*)

Today, we're beginning a time of the church year we call *Advent*. Advent comes right before Christmas. Now of course we can think about Jesus all year round, but Advent is a special time of year when we can remember him.

We can do something during Advent to help us remember Jesus. We can light candles on an Advent wreath. We start by lighting one candle this Sunday.

Let me ask you a question. How many candles will we light next Sunday? (*Two.*)

We will light two next Sunday, and three the following Sunday, and four the next. And after all the candles are finally lit, we will celebrate Christmas!

So, let's light the first Advent candle. (*Light the candle. You might have one of the older children light the candle for you.*) When we see these candles, let's remember that Jesus is our Lord and our friend.

—M.B.

Second Sunday in Advent

———————————————— • ————————————————

The Gospel: Matthew 3:1-12

Focus: Just as John the Baptist prepared people for the coming of the Savior, we can get ready to celebrate the anniversary of Christ's coming.

Experience: The children will first engage in a discussion that will help them learn about John the Baptist. Then the sermon will look at John's message: prepare for the coming of the Lord.

Preparation: Make a poster that proclaims, "The Savior Is Coming!" When the Gospel is announced, you might say something like, "Today's Gospel tells us about John the Baptist. In the children's sermon we're going to talk about John, so I'm going to ask the children to pay special attention as the Gospel is read."

The Savior Is Coming!

(Have the poster next to you, face down so the children can't see what is on it.)

I brought a poster with me today. I'll show it to you in a minute. But first we're going to talk about John the Baptist.

Today's Gospel tells us about John the Baptist. Do you remember when I was reading about him? John was an interesting character. He lived in a desert. Do you remember what kind of clothes he wore? (*Camel's hair and a leather belt.*) That's really rough clothing—clothing fit for the wilderness! Do you remember what he ate? (*Locusts and wild honey.*) Do you know what a locust is? (*A bug, grasshopper.*) Does that sound like something you would like to eat? The honey is ok, but I'm not sure I'd want to eat locusts! But this is food that John would have found in the wilderness.

John baptized many people. That's why we call him John the Baptist. Does anyone know where John did his baptizing. Did he baptize people in a church? (*No, in the Jordan River.*) John baptized people in the Jordan River. He walked with people out into the river and he baptized them in the water.

John was also a preacher. He was a powerful preacher. When he talked, everybody listened! He told people to stop sinning and get ready. Do you know why John told people to get ready? (*Wait for*

response, "The Savior is coming!" If no one answers, simply continue.)
Now we can look at my poster. (*Hold the poster up for everyone to see.*)
I wrote out John's message. "The Savior Is Coming!" "Get ready,"
John told the people. Be prepared, for God is sending a Savior!

Do you know who this Savior is that John talks about (*Jesus.*)
John told the people about the coming of Jesus. That's what makes
John so important. He told people that Jesus was coming. He
helped people get ready for Jesus.

John's words are still important for us today. Jesus still comes to
be with us. In a few weeks it will be Christmas, and this is what
Christmas is all about. Christmas tells us that Jesus comes to be
with you and me.

And so we can say with John the Baptist, "The Savior is
coming." Let's all say those words together. (*Hold up the poster
again.*) "The Savior is coming." That's good news, isn't it? We too
can prepare and be ready. For Jesus is coming to be with us all.

—M.B.

Third Sunday in Advent
——————————•——————————

The Gospel: Matthew 11:2-11

Focus: John the Baptist had some questions about Jesus. Jesus answered him by pointing out all that Jesus was doing. We too have questions about Jesus. We can have our questions answered by looking to Jesus and seeing all that Jesus has done.

Experience: The children will act out the story in the Gospel reading.

Preparation: You should be familiar with the details of the Gospel so you can narrate as the children act out the story.

Are You the Savior?

This morning we'll act out the Gospel reading. Remember the reading; John the Baptist wants to know if Jesus really is the savior who came from God. Let's see if we can act that out.

I need someone to be John the Baptist. (*Find a volunteer.*) Ok, you are John. Now here's the bad news. You are in prison. Let's have you go over there, off to the side. That's a good place for a prison. (*Have the child stand off to the side.*)

Now we need a couple of prison guards. We need two guards to keep an eye on John. Will you two be guards? Good. You should stand in front of John. (*Have the children stand in front of the child playing John.*) Don't let John escape.

Now we need someone to be a follower of John the Baptist, someone who takes a message from John and speaks that message to Jesus. Who wants to be a messenger? (*Find a volunteer.*) You will? Great. You can go stand by John. (*Direct the child to go over to where John is.*) But don't get too close, because John is in jail.

Now we need someone to play the part of Jesus. (*Have the child playing Jesus stand off to your other side, away from the child playing John the Baptist.*)

I'd like for the rest of you to be disciples of Jesus and the crowd that listens to Jesus. You go and sit by Jesus, and pretend you are listening to him. (*Have all the remaining children go over to where Jesus is and sit around him.*)

Let's begin. The Gospel says that John the Baptist is in prison. He has been preaching God's Word, and he told the king to stop sinning. Well, the king didn't like that, so he threw John in prison.

While John is in prison, he starts to wonder about Jesus. Remember, John baptized Jesus. But now John has some questions. John wonders, "Is Jesus really the Savior?"

One of John's followers visited John in prison. (*Send the child who is playing the messenger to the prison.*) John told his follower to go to Jesus and ask Jesus, "Are you the promised Savior?"

John's follower went to find Jesus. Jesus has been teaching the crowds. (*Turn and look at Jesus and the crowd.*) Jesus, have you been teaching? Good. Crowds, have you been listening? Good.

John's follower went to Jesus. (*Have the child walk over to the child playing Jesus.*) The follower said, "Jesus, John the Baptist wants to know if you are really the savior sent from God." (*Have the child ask, "Are you really the Savior?"*)

Jesus had a special answer. It is in our Gospel reading. Jesus said, "Go and tell John what you hear and see: the blind receive their sight, the lame walk, the lepers are cleansed, the deaf hear, the dead are raised, and the poor have good news brought to them" (Matt. 11:5). (*Have the child say, "Look at what I'm doing."*) John's follower went back to John and told what Jesus had said.

Ok, that's the story. Thank you for acting it out. Please come back here to the middle, and we will talk about what we just did.

In the story, John wondered about Jesus. John wondered, "Is Jesus really the Savior?" So John had a friend ask Jesus, "Are you the Savior?" And Jesus said, "Look at all that I'm doing: healing, raising the dead, preaching good news. These things show that I am the Savior."

That's good for us to know. Sometimes in our lives, we have questions too. We wonder, "Is Jesus really *my* Savior? Does he really love *me*?" When we have questions, it's good to remember all that Jesus has done. He has healed people and preached good news. Jesus has died for you and me, and he's risen from the dead. He's claimed us in baptism. Because Jesus has done all these things, we can be certain that he is our Savior. We also know that Jesus is our Lord and that he loves us very much.

That's the message in today's Gospel. Thank you for helping me tell the story. And remember, Jesus is the Savior who loves you very much.   **—M.B.**

Fourth Sunday in Advent

———————————— • ————————————

The Gospel: Matthew 1:18-25

Focus: Jesus is Emmanuel—the promise of God with us.

Experience: We will discuss God's promise to be always with us through Jesus, God's son and explore with the children what this means for them. The intent is for the children to realize that God's promise of Emmanuel is meant for them.

Preparation: You will need a piece of posterboard and a felt-tip marker.

God Is with Us

Today is the fourth Sunday in Advent. That means that Christmas is getting close. Are any of you getting excited (*Probably yes!*) I know I am excited! What are you getting excited about? (*Allow a little time for the children to talk about things that they are getting excited about as Christmas approaches.*) This is an exciting time of year!

Today we'll talk about one of the exciting things about the coming of Christmas. I'd like to talk with you about a very special word—*Emmanuel*. Have you heard that word? (*Allow them to agree or disagree.*) (*Write "Emmanuel" on the posterboard.*) That's a long name, isn't it. Do you know what the word *Emmanuel* means? (*Give the children a chance to answer.*) It means, "God with us." (*Write "God with us" on the posterboard.*) Jesus is sometimes called Emmanuel. That means that when Jesus was born at Christmas, God came to be with us. And God is still with us. In fact, God is *always* with us.

That's very special! We often think that God is far away from us. We think that God is off somewhere, far, far away. But in Jesus God has come to be with us. Jesus has come here to this earth. That's what Christmas tells us. Jesus was born here on this earth. Even now Jesus still comes to care for us, to forgive us, to watch over us. That's what makes this Advent season so wonderful. We are waiting to celebrate Jesus' birthday!

So, Jesus is God with us. Think about that. God loves you so much that God sent Jesus to watch over you and be with you. How does that make you feel? (*Give the children a chance to answer. Talk about and affirm the answers they give. The children will probably say things like, "That makes me feel special," or "It makes me feel good," or "It means God really cares for me.")*

Thank you for sharing your feelings with me. We all can feel special because God loves each one of us and is with us. Remember, that's God's promise! God has sent Jesus to be Emmanuel. (*Hold up the poster again.*) Emmanuel means God is with us, and that's the good news for today.   **—M.B.**

Christmas Eve

—————————•—————————

The Gospel: Luke 2:1-20

Focus: Christmas is the celebration of Jesus' birth.

Experience: The children will talk about Christmas being Jesus' birthday and will sign a birthday card for Jesus.

Preparation: Make a large birthday card, perhaps by folding a piece of poster board in half. That will make a card large enough to be seen by the congregation and strong enough to stand up by itself. On the outside of the card write, "Happy Birthday, Jesus" with bright colors and large letters. On the inside of the card write "We love you" toward the top of the right-hand side.

Bring some felt-tip pens for the children to use in signing the card. (If possible, use washable markers!)

Happy Birthday, Jesus!

It's Christmas Eve! That's a special time, isn't it? It's a time to celebrate. Do you know what we are celebrating tonight? We're celebrating a birthday. Whose birthday are we celebrating? (*Jesus.*)

That's right. On Christmas we celebrate Jesus' birthday. Jesus was born many years ago in a small town. Do you know what the name of the town was? (*Bethlehem.*)

Very good. Jesus was born in Bethlehem. What's so special about Jesus? Why do we celebrate his birthday? (*Give the children a chance to think and answer. Affirm the answers they give, such as Jesus is our Savior, God's Son, the King.*)

Yes, very good. Jesus is God's Son. He came to earth to be our Savior and our King. He is God's Son, and he loves us very much.

This is Jesus' birthday. When we have birthdays, we sometimes receive birthday cards. Have you ever received cards for your birthday? (*Yes.*)

If this is Jesus' birthday, don't you think he should get a card? I made a card and here it is. (*Show the card to the children.*) The front says, "Happy Birthday, Jesus." On the inside it says, "We love you." I thought we'd all sign the card. Should we do that? Great. Let's all sign our names. Anyone who can't write yet can draw a little something on the card. Let's do that now.

(Let all the children write or draw on the card.)

That's great. Thank you for your help. We'll leave the card standing up here in front of the church. (*Stand the card up in front of the church, visible to the congregation.*) The card will remind us that this is Jesus' birthday.   **—M.B.**

The Nativity of Our Lord—Christmas Day
—————————————•—————————————

The Gospel: Luke 2:1-20

Focus: Jesus is the true gift of Christmas.

Experience: Many children come to worship on Christmas, thinking of gifts and presents. We will use the familiar sight of a wrapped Christmas gift to help the children see Jesus as God's gift to us.

Preparation: Type a note on a piece of paper. The note should read:

> For Christmas I give you my only Son. His name is Jesus.
> He will be your Savior. He will love you every day of your
> life. He will give you eternal life and care for you always.
> Merry Christmas!
> Your heavenly Father

Place the note in a large box and wrap the box with Christmas paper. Put a gift tag on the box. The tag should be addressed to the people of (your congregation), from God.

Place the box under the Christmas tree (if you have one) or somewhere else in the sanctuary before the worship service.

A Christmas Present

Merry Christmas! This is the day we've been waiting for. It's Christmas! Is this a special day? (*Allow children to respond.*) It sure is. It is one of the most special days of the year. I love Christmas, and I'm glad we've come together to worship and celebrate.

Did any of you notice that there is a present under the tree today? There it is, right under the tree. (*Ask one of the children to bring the present to you.*)

There is a tag on this gift. It says, (*read the tag with your congregation's name*). That's us, isn't it? It's all of us gathered here together. And the tag says it's from God. Do you think that God would give us a Christmas gift? Would you help me open it and find out what's inside? (*Allow the children to help unwrap the gift.*)

What's inside here? (*A note. Pull it out.*) Let me read it for you. The note says, (*read the note*).

Christmas is a time when we talk about gifts. It is a time to give gifts and to receive gifts. But the greatest gift of all is the gift that God gave on the first Christmas. God loves us very much—so much that God sent Jesus to be with us. That is why we celebrate today. We give and receive gifts because God has given us the greatest gift of all: Jesus. **—M.B.**

First Sunday after Christmas
———————————————•———————————————

The Gospel: Matthew 2:13-15, 19-23

Focus: God keeps his promises.

Experience: In the weeks preceding this Sunday, the children will have heard the Christmas story numerous times. Now they will have a chance to respond to it themselves. The children will also be reminded that God kept his promises on the first Christmas and God keeps his promises to us.

Preparation: Bring a nativity scene.

God Keeps His Promises

Today's Gospel reading tells us about the first Christmas. We've been talking a lot about the story of that first Christmas. (*Hold up the nativity scene.*) Can you tell me who these people are? (*Point to the various figures and have the children identify them.*)

I'd like to ask you a question. You've all heard this story of Jesus' birth. What do you like best about the story? (*Allow time for the children to answer. Engage the children in a discussion. Ask leading questions like, "What do you like about the angels?" You might also point to the appropriate figures in the nativity scene as the children speak. Be sure to give the children a chance to say what they like best about the Christmas story.*)

Those are all very good answers. Thanks for sharing that.

Do you know what my favorite part of the Christmas story is? I like the fact that all through the story, God keeps his promises. Did you notice that?

God promised Mary that she would have a son. God promised Joseph that the child would be very special. God promised the shepherds and the wise men that they would see the newborn king. God promised the world that he would send a Savior. And you know what? God kept all his promises on that first Christmas.

That's good to know, because God has made some important promises to us too. God promises us that this Jesus who was born is our Savior too. God promises us that he will love us and care for

us. And you know what? God keeps his promises to us too! Jesus is
our Savior, and God does love us and care for us.

So, many special things happened on that first Christmas.
Thanks for talking with me about Christmas. And remember, God
keeps his promises. He kept them on that first Christmas, and God
keeps his promises to us too!   —M.B.

Second Sunday after Christmas

———————————————————— • ————————————————————

The Gospel: John 1:1-18

Focus: Jesus is our light.

Experience: The children will experience being "in the dark" and "in the light" by having the church lights turned off and on.

Preparation: Arrange with the ushers to turn all the church lights off and then on again when you tell them to do so. If the Christmas tree is still lit, make arrangements to unplug it. Plan to have the church as dark as possible.

Our Light

I'm going to start today by asking the ushers to turn off all the lights in the church. (*The ushers turn off all the lights.*)

The lights are off. It looks kind of strange in here, doesn't it? Go ahead and look around. (*Give the children a chance to look.*) It's kind of strange. We're used to the church being bright and cheery. But with the lights off it's kind of gray and dreary in here.

There is still light coming in the windows. Imagine if we had the windows covered. What would it be like in here? (*Dark, scary, strange.*)

Yes, If there were no light, it would be strange, wouldn't it. It would be hard to see. It might be confusing. Without light, things just wouldn't seem right.

Today's Gospel tells us that Jesus is our light. What that means is that if we try to live without Jesus, it's going to be like being in here with no lights. Without Jesus our lives will be kind of gray and dreary. Our lives get confused and lost. Things just aren't right without Jesus.

But the good news is that Jesus is here with us. That's what Christmas is all about. Jesus has come to be with us, and he cares for us. Today's Gospel says that Jesus has come to be light in the darkness. He comes to brighten things and to make things right.

So, let's turn the lights back on. (*Have the ushers turn on all the lights.*) What do you think? That's more like it, isn't it! It's bright. It's cheery. Let's remember, Jesus comes to be our light.   **—M.B.**

The Epiphany of Our Lord (January 6)

The Gospel: Matthew 2:1-12

Focus: The search for Jesus by the Magi introduces our ongoing search to "find" Jesus in worship.

Experience: The children will experience a brief "hide-and-seek" game, looking for a picture of Jesus hidden somewhere in the sanctuary. This will introduce the story of the Magi seeking Jesus after his birth.

Preparation: Prior to worship, hide a picture of the nativity (8x10 minimum) in a place where the children will be able to find it without much difficulty. It may help to have someone "guard" the picture so it is not moved by a well-meaning member. You may need to give clues during the search. You will also need a watch to time the search.

Finding Jesus

How many of you have ever played hide and seek? (*Allow time for the children to respond.*) Before worship began today, I hid a picture of the baby Jesus somewhere in the sanctuary. I want you to find it. I will see how long it takes you. Now, go look for Jesus! (*Allow some time for the children to look. Aid them with directions as necessary. Keep track of how much time it takes them to find the picture.*)

You found it! Very good! Do you know it only took you (*fill in the time*) to play hide-and-seek? Now can you imagine playing hide-and-seek for two years without stopping? (*Allow for responses.*) That's a long, long time!

Well, long ago just after Jesus was born, some men from a land far away wanted to find Jesus. Jesus wasn't really hiding from them. They just didn't know exactly where he was. They left their own land to look for Jesus. It was a long, long trip, but God put a special star in the sky to guide them.

The men finally came to the king of the land where Jesus was born. The king gave them a clue. He said to look in Bethlehem. And do you know, that is exactly where the wise men found Jesus!

Today, in our worship we are celebrating their journey to find Jesus.

Now, where did you find Jesus today? (*Allow time for responses.*) Yes. And we can find Jesus in many other places: in our songs, in our prayers, in our Bible stories, in our friends. We can find Jesus at church, but we can also find Jesus in our homes or even at school. We may not see him, but we feel his love and his power because Jesus is with us.

Let's thank Jesus for being someone we can find. Dear Jesus, we are so glad that you let us find you when we look for you. Help us to remember that you are with us everywhere. Amen. **—C.M.C.**

First Sunday after the Epiphany

————————————— • —————————————

The Gospel: Matthew 3:13-17

Focus: Jesus' baptism shows his acceptance of the mission to be our Savior.

Experience: The older children will be "parents" who give the younger children jobs to do. When some of the children agree to do the work, parents will express their happiness.

Preparation: The children will form two groups, one of older children who can read and another of younger children. Have them stand several feet apart. Have an index card for each "parent" with a simple instruction on it such as these: Make your bed. Pick up your toys. Feed the dog.

I Am Very Happy with You

Let's pretend that those on this side are the parents and these others are the children. (*To the parents:*) I want you to ask one of the children in the other group to do the job on this card I am giving you. We will pretend that they are your children. If your child agrees to do the job, you say, "I am very happy about that." OK? (*Go to the children and tell some of them to say no and some of them to say yes to the job they are given.*)

(*Send the parents one at a time to one of the children, to whom they read their cards: "Clean your room. Wash the dishes. Make your bed." The children will answer as you have instructed them. The parents will say they are happy whenever any children agree to the jobs.*)

Good. Now let's all sit down together. What you just did often happens at home when we do something our parents ask. They tell us how happy they are. Even Jesus' Father in heaven told him how happy he was with Jesus. The day Jesus was baptized, God spoke from heaven and said, "This is my Son, the beloved, with you I am well pleased." God was telling Jesus, "I am very happy with you." I wonder how Jesus felt when he heard those words. What do you think? (*Allow time for responses. They may say he felt good, happy, or proud.*)

Those are good answers. Jesus' baptism showed that he was ready to do the work God wanted him to do as our Savior. God's voice from heaven told Jesus that God was very happy about that. In God's family, every person in the family has important work to do, including you. God wants us to help others and care for them. And just like Jesus, we know God is very happy with us!

—**C.M.C.**

Second Sunday after the Epiphany
—————————————————•—————————————————

The Gospel: John 1:29-41

Focus: Jesus takes away the sin of the world.

Experience: A bag of trash will help the children visualize what Jesus has done for us.

Preparation: Cut shapes from construction paper and in large letters label them: *greed, lying, hate, jealousy, hurting, stealing, cheating,* and so on. Put these shapes in a garbage bag and label the bag *sin.*

Jesus Takes It Away

There are lots of jobs, aren't there? Imagine you are a teacher. What are some of the things you would do? (*Allow time for responses. Affirm what is shared.*) Now imagine being a doctor. What are some of the things you would do? (*Responses.*) Now pretend you are a garbage collector. What are some of the things you would do? (*Responses.*)

Every job is important, but garbage collectors have a very important job. It would be terrible if our garbage just piled up higher and higher at our homes. I'm glad we have so many people who are willing to do this job. But the bag I have here holds one kind of garbage that no garbage collector can haul away. Can you guess what it is? (*Allow time for responses, but do not expect anyone to answer correctly.*) Let me show you some of it. (*Pull pieces of the labeled trash out one at a time and read the labels.*) Here is lying. And greed. And here is hate. All this garbage has one name. Do you know what that is? (*Reveal this label and allow for responses.*) These are all names of different kinds of sin. And no human garbage collector could ever take it away. But do you know who can take sin away? (*Jesus!*)

That is right! John the Baptist tells us that Jesus "takes away the sin of the world" (John 1:29). Sin ruins everything. We don't feel happy when selfishness, meanness, hate, and other sins are in our lives. Sin makes us miserable. And sin keeps us from being friends with God. But Jesus was willing to come and take away this garbage of sin. I'm so glad he did that! Now our lives can become clean and fresh. And we can have God as our friend. Let's thank Jesus right now for taking away our sin. (*Pray a prayer of thanks.*)

—C.M.C.

Third Sunday after the Epiphany

The Gospel: Matthew 4:12-23

Focus: We need to follow Jesus.

Experience: By playing two different versions of "follow the leader," the children will experience the importance of followers to the success of the game. This will point to the importance of following Jesus, our leader.

Follow the Leader

Have you ever played follow the leader? (*Allow time for responses.*) Well, today I want to teach you a new way to play it. Now, you all sit here and watch me. (*Alone, the leader walks, skips, hops, and jumps around the sanctuary and back to the children in front.*) There. Did you like playing follow the leader with me? (*Allow for responses. They probably didn't like it.*)

It didn't work out very well, did it? You didn't get to do anything, did you? Let's try it again, but this time, you follow me and do what I do! (*Children follow the leader around the sanctuary and back to front.*) That was a lot better, wasn't it?

We just proved that to play follow the leader takes more than just a leader. It takes followers, too. When Jesus wanted to lead his disciples, he called them to follow him. Peter and John and the others did follow him. They followed and they learned and they taught others and they started the church that we still have today.

You and I can follow Jesus too. We follow Jesus in many ways: when we come to church and pray and love and care for others. Let's pray now. Jesus, thank you for asking us to follow you. We know you are a good leader. Help us to follow where you lead us. Amen. **—C.M.C.**

Fourth Sunday after the Epiphany

————————————— • —————————————

The Gospel: Matthew 5:1-12

Focus: God blesses us in life.

Experience: A sneezing pastor will get children to say "God bless you." This leads into the discussion of blessings.

God Bless You!

I have a bad case of the sneezes today. (*Aachoo!*) I don't (*aachoo!*) know if I can (*aachoo!*) talk to you today (*aachoo!*). One nice thing (*aachoo!*) about sneezing is what people say (*aachoo!*) when you sneeze. Do you know (*aachoo!*) what that is (*aachoo!*)? (*Allow time for responses.*) That's right. Many people say "God bless you." I like it when (*aachoo!*) people say, "God bless you." (*Try to get children saying this every time you sneeze now.*) Sometimes (*aachoo!*) when no one says it (*aachoo!*), I say, "God bless you" to myself (*aachoo!*)!

Jesus liked to say "God bless you" too. One day, Jesus was telling his followers about God's kingdom. He said "Bless you," even though they weren't sneezing! He said things like, "If you show mercy to others, God will bless you with mercy," and, "If you are sad, God will bless you with comfort."

"God bless you" really means, "May God give you the good gifts that you need." Can you name some of the good gifts God has given you to enjoy in your life? (*Allow time for responses such as family, friends, pets, toys.*) Our lives are full of these gifts, aren't they? These gifts are our blessings. Isn't it wonderful to have a God who blesses us so much, even when we don't sneeze? And when we do? (*Aachoo!*)   —C.M.C.

Fifth Sunday after the Epiphany
—————————————————— • ——————————————————

The Gospel: Matthew 5:13-20

Focus: Jesus says we are the light of the world. Jesus is the source of that light.

Experience: The children will overcome the problem of a light that won't work and begin to see how we cannot work as lights unless we overcome the same problems with Jesus' help.

Preparation: Bring a small table lamp or desk lamp. Give the sermon from somewhere near an electrical outlet, or use an extension cord so that you can plug in the lamp during the sermon.

The Light of the World

I want you to see something I think is very pretty. (*Show the lamp.*) It helps me in many ways. Who can guess some ways this lamp can help me? (*Allow responses.*) That's right. It can help me read or to see better in a dark room. It can help me work. It can keep me from being afraid of the dark.

But I have a little problem. Let me show you. I flip the switch, but nothing happens. What do you think might be wrong? (*Allow time for responses. Affirm their ideas and test them out. If no one suggests it, pull the plug at the end of the cord toward you until the children can see that it's not plugged in.*) Of course! In order to work, the lamp needs to be plugged into an electrical outlet. (*Plug it in and turn it on.*) There, that's much better, isn't it?

When Jesus said, "You are the light of the world," he meant that we are something like this lamp. Jesus wants us to shine by showing love to others and caring for them. Just like the outlet gave power to the lamp, Jesus helps us and gives us power. Without Jesus' help, we are like a lamp that isn't plugged in. But when we ask Jesus to give us power, he helps us. Then we can love others and care for them.

So when you have a chance to do something good for someone, ask Jesus to give you the power you need to do it. He will help you to shine!   —C.M.C.

Sixth Sunday after the Epiphany
———————————————— • ————————————————

The Gospel: Matthew 5:20-37

Focus: Jesus teaches us how to get along well with others and stay out of trouble.

Experience: By playing and singing "London Bridge," the children will get to consider being in jail. Jesus' words teach us how to live together in a loving community.

Preparation: Make room to play this game.

The Lesson of "London Bridge"

Do you know the song "London Bridge Is Falling Down"? (*Allow responses.*) Then let's sing it! Line up, and we'll have you two be the bridge. The rest can walk through in a circle as we sing.

> *London Bridge is falling down, falling down, falling down.*
> *London Bridge is falling down. My fair lady.*
> *Here's the prisoner we have caught, we have caught, we have caught.*
> *Here's the prisoner we have caught. My fair lady.*
> *Take the key and lock her up, lock her up, lock her up.*
> *Take the key and lock her up. My fair lady.*

(*Play for a minute.*) In that song-game, we "Take the key and lock her up." But we are just pretending, aren't we? I don't think it would be any fun at all if I was really locked up in jail. I don't think I would be laughing. How would you feel if that happened to you? (*Affirm all responses.*)

Jesus loves us and wants us to get along with one another. He told us two very good ways to stay out of trouble: keep control of what you think and what you do. Can you think of any places where you could do those two things? (*Allow time for responses such as home, school, the playground.*) Yes. The best place to start doing that is right at home with your own family—then in school and in your neighborhood. Even when you feel angry, Jesus wants you to control your actions, and Jesus will help you to do this. Just ask him to help you. Then you won't have to worry about getting locked up, except on London Bridge! Now let's thank Jesus for caring enough about us to give us these helpful words. —**C.M.C.**

Seventh Sunday after the Epiphany
———————————————•———————————————

The Gospel: Matthew 5:38-48

Focus: Jesus' teaching, "love your enemies," is difficult for children and adults. But it is important for us to try to do what Jesus wants us to do.

Experience: The children will recall playing war, express feelings about real war, and learn a new way to act toward enemies.

Turning Enemies into Friends

When I was growing up, one of the games I played with my friends was war. Another was cowboys and Indians. Another was police and robbers. Have you played any games like that? (*Allow time for responses.*) These games are just pretend, but one strange thing about these games is that friends pretend to be enemies so they can be on opposite sides. And then they pretend to hurt each other. They aren't really enemies. But in our world, many people are real enemies. They fight with each other. How do you think God feels about that? (*Allow time for responses and affirm them.*)

You're probably right. I have an idea about all this fighting. What if all the real enemies pretended to be friends? Instead of fighting, they could play "friends." If real enemies played friends long enough, they might become real friends and stop being enemies! That would be good, wouldn't it?

My idea may not work, but we can help make our world more peaceful by loving other people. Jesus even wants us to love people who don't love us. That is what God does, and Jesus did it too. Who knows? They just might become your real friends!

So not only can we make new friends, but we can also be happy that we already have some friends right here in church. Look around. Some of your friends are about your age, some younger, and some older. As you go back to where you were sitting, or right up here among the children, find someone, old or young, and tell them "I'm glad you are my friend." Then hug them or put your arm around their shoulders or shake their hands. We thank God for our friends!   **—C.M.C.**

Eighth Sunday after the Epiphany

———————————— • ————————————

The Gospel: Matthew 6:24-34

Focus: Jesus says we cannot serve God and another master at the same time. We must choose to serve God only.

Experience: The children will feel the pull between two "masters"—the pastor or other leader and the organist, both of whom want the children to obey them. It will force the children to choose who they will listen to.

Who Will You Listen to?

(*Invite the children to come up for the children's sermon. As the children begin to assemble with the leader, another voice—the choir director or organist says, "Kids, come over here and we will sing a song together." The kids may start to move from pastor to the other person. Ask them to come back to you because you want to tell them a story. Then have the other person make another appeal. The children may be in two or three groups, or they may be somewhere in between.*)

This is confusing, isn't it? (*Allow time for responses.*) Is it hard to know who you should listen to? (*Allow time for responses.*)

We were trying to show you what Jesus meant when he said that we cannot serve two masters. You could not do what both of us asked at the same time. We wanted you to do different things in different places at the same time. If we had been serious, you would have had to decide which one of us you would listen to. Well, Jesus was serious when he told his followers that they could only serve one master at a time. And the best master to serve is the one Jesus said to serve. Do you know who that is? (*Allow time for responses. Help them to discover the answer is God.*) Jesus wants us to serve God. But how can we learn what God wants us to do? How can we learn to serve? (*Allow time for responses such as pray, go to church, Sunday school, parents, and so on. Affirm their responses.*) Sunday school and church, youth groups, and your parents will all help you learn to listen to God as your master. And remember to pray to God when you are wondering what to do because God loves you very much. God wants to help you.   **—C.M.C.**

The Transfiguration of Our Lord —
Last Sunday After the Epiphany

—————————————— • ——————————————

The Gospel: Matthew 17:1-9

Focus: The change Jesus underwent revealed something about his true nature.

Experience: By putting on new clothing, the children will be changed—or transfigured—in front of the congregation. This can help explain what happened to Jesus on the Mount of Transfiguration.

Preparation: You will need several shopping bags containing two or three items of large, loose clothing for each child (overcoats, robes, hats).

What a Change!

I want you to help me teach our congregation about a very special time in Jesus' life. It is called the *transfiguration*. That is a big word that means a big change takes place. So I want you to change in front of everyone. I want you to have a transfiguration right here. Each of you take a bag, but don't open it yet. When I say, *Transfigure!* I want you to open the bag and put on whatever is in it. Ready? Transfigure! (*Encourage the children to rapidly put on the clothing in the bags.*)

Look at these children! None of them look like they did a few seconds ago. That change was so fast! You all look very different. But you are still you, aren't you? (*Allow responses.*)

This is what happened to Jesus! He took some close friends up on a mountain one day. And right before their eyes, he was changed—transfigured! It was not because Jesus put on different clothes like you did. His own clothing became as white as light and his own face shined like the sun! That didn't happen to any of you, but it happened to Jesus. He was still Jesus, but his friends now knew that he was not just a human being. They knew Jesus was the Son of God.

All right, now you can "transfigure" back again. Thank you for coming up today.   **—C.M.C.**

First Sunday in Lent

————————————•————————————

The Gospel: Matthew 4:1-11

Focus: Temptation is built on false promises.

Experience: Through a demonstration of temptation, children will learn that it is often difficult to separate the lie of temptation from the half-truths that come with it.

Preparation: Bring a billfold with a one-, five-, and ten-dollar bill in it.

I'll Give You What You Want

Our Bible story tells us that the devil tempted Jesus. That means that the devil tried to talk Jesus into doing something bad. Let's play a game that will show you how temptation works.

First we need to think of something bad. Do you think it would be bad if you told a lie about something? (*Allow time for responses.*) Even if it seems like a small lie, we know it is wrong to lie. When we lie, sometimes it gets us in trouble. Sometimes our lies can get others in trouble. It is wrong to lie.

Now the second part of temptation is for me to try to talk you into doing something you know is wrong. Since at this moment you have no reason to want to tell a lie, what would make you want to do it? Let's see (*take out the billfold*), if someone gave you a dollar if you would tell a lie, would you tell one? Remember, you might get into trouble. (*Show the dollar.*) What about five? (*Show it.*) Ten? (*Show the ten.*) Would you do it for a hundred dollars? A thousand? How about a million dollars? Remember, you may get into trouble and you know it is wrong to lie. (*Allow the children to respond. Some may give in easily. Some will try to do the "right thing." Try your best to tempt them.*)

Well, since we were only playing a game, I won't give anyone any money. And I want to remind you that it is wrong to lie. But did you notice something? After awhile I didn't show you the money I offered. Do you know why? That's right—I didn't have that much money. That's what temptation does. It offers you something that it can't give to you.

In our Bible story, the devil offered Jesus the whole world if Jesus would worship him. The devil doesn't own the world—God does. But the devil offered it anyway.

The devil also tempts us and offers us rewards that he can't give. He tells us that if we say bad things about others, people will think we are better than others. But it doesn't really work. The devil tells people that if they use drugs and alcohol, these things will make them happy—but it doesn't happen that way.

Jesus said no! to Satan. He knew he didn't have to worship the devil to own the world. Instead, Jesus loves all the people of the world. He's our Savior. He forgives our sins and protects us from things that hurt us. Jesus was tempted, but didn't sin. He said no. When we are tempted, Jesus can help us to say no too.   —E.W.

Second Sunday in Lent
———————————————•———————————————

The Gospel: John 4:5-26

Focus: There is a difference between meeting Jesus and living with him. Jesus offers us true friendship.

Experience: We will talk about the human need for water and compare it to God's blessings to us in Holy Baptism.

Preparation:—Bring a bottle of water and a picture of a water fountain. Or, if practical, move the group to be near a drinking fountain.

A Drink That Lasts and Lasts

Let's pretend that your family is going for a week of vacation at a camp. (*Name a farm, park, island, or something that would be remote.*) You'd have to take along food to last the whole week. But you wouldn't have to take water because it is already there.

When you get to camp you find this: one bottle of water. (Show it.) Would that be enough for your family for a whole week? (*Allow time for responses.*) No way! You would need a supply of water like this. (*Show the picture or remind them of a nearby drinking fountain.*) With a supply of water like this, everyone could get a drink at any time.

Jesus met a woman who went to a well to get a big jar of water. He told her that she needed more than one day's supply of water. She needed a supply of water that would last forever. The woman didn't know what he meant. Jesus explained, "Everyone who drinks of this water will be thirsty again, but those who drink of the water that I will give them will never be thirsty. The water that I will give will become in them a spring of water gushing up to eternal life" (John 4:13-14).

Jesus says that when you take a drink of water, you will get thirsty again. And that's true about regular water. But then Jesus offers us something special. It is not water for our body, but it is a message for our lives. The message is that Jesus gives us new life every day.

Our baptism reminds us of that new life. (*Show water in baptismal font or point to it. If there is a baptism in the same worship service, connect it with the children's sermon.*) The water we use in baptism doesn't last long. It dries up. But God's Word, God's promises, in baptism last all of our lives. God's word tells us that God loves us and wants us to be part of his family. This word of God is a promise to us that God will be with us every day of our lives. And this gift is not just for the day we were baptized. It continues as God lives with us always.   **—E.W.**

Third Sunday in Lent
————————————————————— • —————————————————————

The Gospel: John 9:31-41

Focus: When Jesus lived on earth, many people looked at him but did not see that he was the Son of God living with them. Today we may hear about him but not hear him. This sermon is to help children to know that Jesus is their friend and Savior.

Experience: The children will be challenged to use their eyes to look for something and will see that not all things that can be seen are obvious at once.

Preparation: Before the worship service, place a small cross (color and size so that it can be seen but does not automatically get everyone's attention) in a visible, but not obvious place.

Look and See

Do you see anything different in the church today? (*They may name some obvious things. Keep discussion at this point brief.*) There is something new in the church. Can you see it? (*If someone spots the cross, reward the keen sense of observation and direct others to it.*) I can see it because I know it is there. (*Point first to the general area where the cross is located. Continue to be more specific until all the children see it. If practical move to stand near the cross.*) See, the cross is not hidden. But you need to know where to look in order to see it.

Sometimes we look at things but do not see them because we don't pay any attention. This also happened when Jesus lived on earth. Lots of people saw him, and lots of them didn't know that he was the Savior. One man had been blind from the time he was born. Of course, he couldn't see Jesus, but he learned about the Savior. And Jesus healed him. Then the man could see for the first time in his life.

In one way the man who had been blind could see Jesus in the same way as all others. But he saw more than many of the others saw. He knew that Jesus was God's Son. He knew Jesus loved him and would continue to help him. The others looked at Jesus but did not see what the man who had been blind saw.

Now that you have looked at this cross, it is easy for you to see it. You know where to look. You can also know that Jesus is with you all the time when you know who he is. He is the Savior who gave his life for you. He listens to your prayers. He loves you. You can see him, not with your eyes, but with your heart.   —E.W.

Fourth Sunday in Lent
—————————————————— • ——————————————————

The Gospel: Matthew 20:17-28

Focus: Jesus tells us our status in life is a gift from him.

Experience: Lining up children to represent society's view of status offers a way to contrast the Christian view of status.

Jesus Was the Last in Line

Has anyone asked you to line up? (*Allow for responses.*) There are lots of reasons to line up. When you're standing in line, would you rather be at the front of the line, or the back of the line? (*Most will say "front."*) The people at the front of the line sometimes think they're more important than those at the back of the line.

Let's make a line of the people who were important during the time Jesus lived on earth. One of the most important leaders was Pilate. He was Rome's governor. He lived in a big house with guards. He was in charge of the army. So Pilate will be first in line. (*Ask one child to start the line.*)

Then Herod would be next. He was a king. He had to check things out with Pilate, but he was still king. (*Another child is Herod.*) Then there was the high priest (*another child*), and after him were the teachers of the law (*two children*), then the teachers who were called rabbis (*two more children*).

Then there were many other people who didn't think they were very important. They were fishermen, carpenters, farmers, and workers. (*Have all the other children stand at the back of the line, except for one.*)

When Jesus grew up, everyone knew who was important and who was not important. Where do you think Jesus stood in this line? We know he is important. But he is important because he went to this (*back*) end of the line. He came to be with the lonely people, the poor, the sick, the ones no one else liked. Because he cared about sinners, the people at the front of the line didn't like him. They killed him. But you know the rest of the story. He came back to life, and he still is alive today.

Jesus told us that if we want to be great, we won't try to get to the front of the line. He says that people who boss others and who care only for themselves are not the most important. He says it is more important to help people at the end of the line. Jesus said, "Whoever wishes to be great among you must be your servant, and whoever wishes to be first among you must be your slave" (Matt. 20:26-27).

The good news is that Jesus loves us and comes to us where we are so he can help us. Here's some more good news. because Jesus is with us, we can help others. We can go to where people need us. (*Bring the front of the line toward the back and join hands to form a circle.*) Jesus asks us all to help one another.   **—E.W.**

Fifth Sunday in Lent

———————————————— • ————————————————

The Gospel: John 11:47-53

Focus: The story of Lazarus gets us ready to celebrate the resurrection of Christ.

Experience: This sermon helps the children see that Jesus had to die before he could win the battle against death.

Let's Go Look for Jesus

Let's go look for Jesus. Where shall we look? (*Allow time for responses. Point to the crucifix, cross, or other reminders of Jesus in the building.*) Are those things really Jesus? (*No.*) Then where can we find him? (*Allow time for responses.*) That's right. We can find stories about Jesus in the Bible. These stories are the clues that we use to find Jesus today. The stories about Jesus tell how he lived with people long ago. From these we find out how he lives with us today.

For example, in the eleventh chapter of John we read about Jesus and Lazarus. Do you remember anything about Lazarus? (*Allow time for responses.*) Lazarus was Jesus' friend. Lazarus died, but four days later Jesus went out to the cemetery and told Lazarus to get up and come out of his grave. And Lazarus did.

That's a great story! In two weeks we are going to celebrate Easter. What great thing happened on the first Easter? (*Allow time for responses. Affirm what is shared.*) Jesus died on the cross. Isn't that strange? Jesus did good things and helped people. He was the "good guy" in all the stories. After he brought Lazarus back to life, some people were happy and believed in him.

But do you know what? Some people got angry about it. They weren't glad that Lazarus was alive again. They were mad. They said Jesus was causing problems by doing things like that. So they went out looking for Jesus. They thought what he was doing was wrong, and they wanted to kill him.

Even though Jesus had to die, we know that on Easter he rose up out of his grave and became alive again. And Jesus lives with us right now.

Today we also look for Jesus because we love him. As we read the stories in the Bible about Jesus, we will see that he died for us. On Easter Sunday we will look for Jesus and hear that he came back to life. And Jesus looks for *us* every day because he loves us and wants to be with us.   **—E.W.**

Sunday of the Passion—Palm Sunday
———————————— • ————————————

The Gospel: Matthew 27:11-54

Focus: Jesus took the punishment for something he did not do.

Experience: By acting out a modern trial, the children will experience what it means when we say he died in our place.

Preparation: Be sure you know enough of the children's names so you can address them by name where directions indicate child #1, child #2.

Who Did It?

Do you know what a trial is? It's a way we use to decide if someone is innocent or guilty. We have trials in court to find out if people have broken the law. The trials ask, "Who did it?"

Jesus had a trial. People accused him of doing bad things. We know he is God's Son, and he never did anything wrong. Yet he was found guilty and was killed.

Let's pretend to have a trial here to help us see why Jesus was found guilty and killed. First we need a crime. We will pretend— remember, this is only pretend—that (child #1) (*pick a child that is secure and old enough to understand that he or she is not being accused*) stole a candy bar from the store. Let's pretend that you took the candy but that no one knows you did it.

Now, let's pretend someone who works in the store saw a bunch of kids at the candy counter and knows the candy bar was stolen. But he accuses the wrong kid. He said (child #2) took it (*choose a different child*). He calls the police, and they ask you questions. (*Ask child #2 to sit on a chair or on the floor alone.*)

How can (child #2) prove he or she didn't do it? (*Let the children discuss.*) But let's pretend these two children are friends. Let's pretend (child #2) doesn't want to tattle on a friend and doesn't say anything. (Child #2) lets others think he or she did it. (Child #2) will be punished for what someone else did. (*Reassure both children that this was just pretend and they were good actors.*)

Our Bible story says Jesus was on trial. He took the punishment even though he had done nothing wrong. He knows that *we are* the people who have sinned, not him. But Jesus is our friend. He does not want us to be punished. So he has taken the punishment for us. The Bible says he did not defend himself. He let the judge think he was guilty. Jesus took our punishment for what we did wrong.

Jesus died for us because he wanted to, but then he rose again. Jesus is alive! He loves us and wants to help us. We can celebrate because he has done this for us.   **—E.W.**

The Resurrection of Our Lord—Easter Day

———————————— • ————————————

The Gospel: John 29:1-9 (10-18)

Focus: Seeing does not always mean believing.

Experience: The children will experience what it is like to think they are seeing one thing when really they are seeing another.

Preparation: Bring an egg carton containing one hard-boiled, uncolored egg and a bowl or container to drop it into.

Seeing Is Not Believing

Does anyone know what day it is today? (*Allow time for responses.*) That's right—it's Easter! Do you know why we celebrate Easter in our church? (*Field, Repeat, and affirm responses. Be ready for some responses about Easter eggs and bunnies. Help the children understand that we are celebrating the good news that Jesus is alive again.*)

Does anyone know what the word *resurrection* means? (*Allow time for responses and affirm them.*) Resurrection means "coming back to life." Jesus was killed on the cross on Good Friday. But three days later, on Easter Sunday, he came back to life.

Today we are going to figure out how one of Jesus' best friends, Mary, didn't recognize him after he died and came back to life. Let's see how that could be.

Did any of you find Easter eggs today? (*Allow time for responses.*) What do Easter eggs look like? (*Responses.*) Well, I got this egg out of my refrigerator this morning. (*Open up the carton, carefully remove the hard-boiled egg*) Is it an Easter egg? (*Not really. It looks like any other egg.*) If we dropped this egg, what would happen? (*Crack, break.*) If we dropped it from this high (*a few inches*), what would happen? (*Not much—maybe a crack.*) What if we dropped it from this high (*a couple feet*)? (*It would break.*) What if we dropped it from way up here? (*It would splatter.*) Does anybody want to drop it? (*If there's a volunteer, let him or her drop it into the bowl or container from a height sufficient to break the shell. If no one volunteers, drop it yourself.*) What happened? (*Allow time for responses.*) Why do you suppose that happened? (*Some will not know. Some will guess that it has been cooked, it is a hard-boiled egg*). Isn't that strange? You saw the egg. But since you thought it was raw, you thought it would break. You didn't see this egg for what it is: a cooked egg.

That's like what happened to Mary, Jesus' friend. She saw Jesus die, so she thought he was dead. Then when she first saw him on Easter, she didn't recognize him because she thought he was dead. It wasn't until he called her name that she knew he was alive again—risen from the dead. How happy we are at Easter because Jesus is alive!   **—L.S. and G.W.**

Second Sunday of Easter

————————— • —————————

The Gospel: John 20:19-31

Focus: Jesus brings us peace that we can share with others.

Experience: The children will hear how Jesus came to give peace to his disciples and to them. They will also have a chance to share that peace with others.

A Surprise Visitor

I really enjoy it when people surprise me with a visit. Do you like surprise visitors? (*Allow responses.*) Who is your favorite visitor? (*Responses.*)

Suppose one day we were all together and we heard a knock at the door. It would be fun to have a visitor, wouldn't it? (*Responses.*) Well, one day the disciples had a surprise visitor. They were all together, but they weren't happy. They were sad. Jesus had died, and they were afraid. The felt alone without him. They didn't know what to do. So they just locked the doors and hid together.

Jesus came into the room and surprised them all. He said, "Peace be with you" (John 20:19). The disciples couldn't believe it. They had seen Jesus die on the cross, but here he was—alive again. Jesus knew that his disciples were feeling lost and afraid, and he wanted to help them. So he told them again, "Peace be with you. As the Father has sent me, so I send you" (John 20:21). Jesus' surprise visit made his disciples feel happy. They knew then that they would not be alone. They knew that Jesus was still with them and that he still loved them.

Can you tell me some times when you have felt alone? (*Responses will vary. Perhaps at bedtime, when they are sick, when they are home by themselves, when they have been lost. Affirm their responses.*) There are many times in our lives when we will be alone or feel alone. But, just like the disciples, we know that Jesus is still with us and that he still loves us. But we don't usually see Jesus as the disciples did. How can we feel that Jesus is with us if we can't see him? (*Prayer, reading the Bible, talking to parents or friends or the pastor.*) That's right. In all these ways, Jesus still comes to be with us and to help us. Jesus says to us, "Peace be with you."

There is a way that we can share Jesus' peace with others too. I will start by saying, "The peace of the Lord be with you," and then you can say, "And also with you." Let's practice that. (*Lead the responses.*) Then I would like you to share the peace of Jesus with the rest of the congregation. You can just say, "The peace of the Lord" and smile at someone or you can shake their hand or give them a hug or a kiss. You can decide the best way for you to share God's peace with the rest of the congregation, but I don't want you to sit down until each of the people sitting out there has gotten a handshake, or a smile, a hug, or something. Ready? Let's go! (*Begin by saying "The peace of the Lord be with you." Then encourage the children and adults to say, "And also with you." Then say, "Let us share that peace with one another." You may need to lead the way toward the back of the church so that the children don't all crowd around to the front. Encourage the adults also to "pass the peace" among themselves.*)—**L.S. and G.W.**

Third Sunday of Easter
————————————————————— • —————————————————————

The Gospel: Luke 24:13-35

Focus: The gift of Holy Communion has been given to us to remind us of who Jesus is, as well as what he said and did.

Experience: By looking at pictures and listening to stories the children will gain an understanding of what remembrance means.

Preparation: Bring a picture of your own grandmother or grandfather or some person important to you, as well as Communion bread and wine.

Remembering Jesus

I'm glad you came up today. We are going to talk about remembering. What do you think it means to remember something? (*Allow time for responses. Affirm what is shared.*) Remembering means to bring something back into your mind and think about again.

What does this look like (*hold up the picture*)? (*Allow responses.*) Right. It's a picture. It's a picture of (*give name and relationship. Then tell some things you remember about this person.*)

When people are important to us, we like to remember them, and pictures can help us remember.

Jesus wants us to remember him too. There's just one problem. Were any of us alive when Jesus lived on earth? (*No.*) So we don't remember what *we* used to do with Jesus, do we? (*No.*) No, but we remember Jesus by doing what he did with his disciples. Does anyone remember what that is? (*Allow time for responses.*) We call it Holy Communion. Right before he died, Jesus ate a meal of bread and wine (*show the communion bread and wine*) with his disciples, and he told them to eat that meal to remember him. So when we have Communion, we remember Jesus by eating bread (*show*) and drinking wine (*show*) just like he did with his disciples.

We have never seen Jesus, but we can remember him when we see the bread and wine of Holy Communion. (*You may want to take a moment to state your congregation's Communion practice. If young children are not included, you may wish to conclude, "we remember Jesus, even when we don't take the bread and wine of Communion, because we listen to the Bible and know we are part of Jesus' family, the church."*)

—L.S. and G.W.

Fourth Sunday of Easter

———————————— • ————————————

The Gospel: John 10:1-10

Focus: Jesus comes to us as a shepherd, the one who will do *anything* to protect his flock from harm.

Experience: This message will help the children feel the dedicated and protective presence of Jesus.

Preparation: Bring a picture of a herd of sheep or sheep in a pen.

Jesus, Our Shepherd

I'm very glad you came up. Today we're going to solve a mystery. We'll call it the mystery of the shepherd and the thief. Who knows what these are? (*Show the picture. Allow time for responses.*) Right. They're sheep. They live in groups called—what? (*Flocks.*) That's right. They live in flocks. And what do we call the people who take care of sheep? (*Shepherds.*) Yes. Shepherds care for sheep.

Now, does anyone know what a thief is? (*Allow for responses. Help them define a thief as someone who takes something that does not belong to that person.*)

Now, let's suppose we have two people standing side by side (*choose two children to stand*). They look pretty much alike. But one is a shepherd who takes care of sheep and one is a thief who wants to steal the sheep. Let's see how we can tell which one is which. (*Discuss the similarities between the two: similar height, clothes, color of hair. Ask, "Can we tell which one is the shepherd and which one is the thief?" Help the children understand that they can't yet tell who is the shepherd.*)

Well, let's pretend they are both carrying those curved sticks that shepherds carry. Can we tell yet? (*No.*) Well, if we can't recognize the shepherd by his or her clothes, how can we tell? Here is a clue: If one is standing by the gate of the sheep pen, caring for the sheep, but one is *sneaking* in over the fence, which one do you think is the thief? (*Allow and affirm responses.*) Right! You solved the mystery. (*Thank the two children and reassure "the thief" that he or she is not a thief, just a good actor.*) Jesus tells us in today's Gospel that we are like sheep and he is like a shepherd taking care of us. Just as the shepherd cares for the sheep, Jesus cares for us. **—L.S. and G.W.**

Fifth Sunday of Easter
————————————————•————————————————

The Gospel: John 14:1-12

Focus: Jesus' acts of healing, love, mercy, kindness, and forgiveness reveal God to us.

Experience: We learn a lot about people by what they do, and we learn about God by observing what Jesus did.

Preparation: Although no specific preparation is necessary, you could bring items used by people in the professions you discuss in this week's children's sermon.

Learning About God

Last week we solved a mystery, and this week we're going to solve another one. This is one that Jesus' disciples couldn't solve. But first, let's play a game. I'm going to tell you something that someone does in their work, and you can tell me what that job is called.

Ready? This person teaches children. What is the job called? (*Teacher.*) Teacher, right! You're pretty good at this already. Now, let's try another one. This person helps you get well. (*Doctor or nurse would be fine, so would mom or dad.*) Great! How about someone who cuts hair? (*Barber or hairdresser.*) How about someone who puts out fires? (*Firefighters.*) You're doing great! Here's the last one. Someone who wears a badge and keeps our neighborhoods safe. (*Police officer.*) Very, very good. You know about people because you see what they do.

Now let's look at the mystery the disciples could not solve. The disciples had seen all the things that Jesus did. Does anyone remember any of them? (*If no one does, just go on.*) Jesus raised people from the dead. He helped blind people to see. He taught people about God. He healed people who were sick. The disciples saw everything Jesus did. But the disciples didn't just want to see Jesus; they wanted to see God. And they asked Jesus to show God to them. Jesus said, "Whoever has seen me has seen the Father (John 14:9). Jesus was telling his disciples, "Watch what I do and you will learn about God."

We can do the same thing. We have never seen God, but we can know about God by learning what Jesus has done. **—L.S. and G.W.**

Sixth Sunday of Easter
—————————————— • ——————————————

The Gospel: John 14:15-21

Focus: Jesus sent the Holy Spirit to comfort us and to remind us of all the things Jesus said and did while he was alive.

Exercise: Children will gain a sense of being alone and being comforted by the presence of the Holy Spirit.

Preparation: Bring a picnic basket or cooler.

The Comforter

Today we're going to pretend we're going on a picnic. Where should we go? (*Allow time for responses.*) Those are very good suggestions! Let's pretend that we're going on a picnic at (*use one of the responses*). I brought this (*show the cooler or picnic basket*). What food should we take? (*Allow time for responses and affirm what is suggested.*) Great! Should we take any toys or games? (*Allow time for responses.*)

Now let's pretend it's almost dark. We've eaten all our food. We played and had fun together. We're tired and it's time to go home. So we pack up the car. There's so much stuff in it that I think you're in the car too, but you're still playing outside. Let's pretend it's getting dark and I don't see you, so I drive away. What would you do? (*Allow time for responses.*) How would you feel? (*Allow time for responses. Try to be reassuring if anyone seems frightened.*)

Now, pretend that I just realized you were still at the picnic grounds, so I'm driving back to get you just as fast as I can. How would you feel when you saw me coming back to get you? (*Allow for responses. Focus on the feelings of relief and comfort.*)

No one likes to be left alone. Jesus knew that. That's why he promised his disciples that when he died he would not leave them alone. And Jesus kept his promise. He sent the Holy Spirit to be with them. The Holy Spirit would help the disciples to feel safe when they were afraid, and to feel peace when they were alone.

Jesus hasn't left us alone either. He has given us the Holy Spirit too. We can't see the Holy Spirit, the Spirit of God, but Jesus says the Holy Spirit is with us to help us and to make us feel safe. It's good to know God is always with us!   **—L.S. and G.W.**

Seventh Sunday of Easter

————————————— • —————————————

The Gospel: John 17:1-11

Focus: The protection of God overrides the threat of the world.

Experience: The purpose of this message is to demonstrate protection and to present the idea that God protects us as a church.

Preparation: Bring a sweater, umbrella, and sunscreen (or three other items of protection) and a doll.

Protection

Does anyone know what it means to protect something? (*Allow time for responses. Affirm what is shared.*) To protect means to keep someone or something safe.

I brought a sweater, an umbrella, and some sunscreen with me today. Suppose you were taking care of a little baby (*hold up the doll*). Which one of these would you use to protect the baby from the rain? (*Umbrella.*) Which would you use to protect the baby from the cold? (*Sweater.*) What would you use to protect the baby from sunburn? (*Sunscreen.*) Very good. You are protecting this baby very well. But could this baby protect herself? (*No.*) You're right. She needs help.

Even big people like us need help sometimes. Right before Jesus died, he asked God to protect the church. He wasn't talking about buildings or parking lots or bricks or windows. He was talking about the believers—the people who believe in him. Us. Jesus asked God to protect and take care of us. Why do you think Jesus asked God to take care of us? (*Allow time for responses.*) Jesus asked God to take care of us because he loves us. He also knows that every day we have to make choices, and sometimes it's hard to do the right thing. So if it's ever hard for you to do the right thing, you can know that God is right there helping and protecting *you* just like you protected this baby. That's really good news!

—L.S. and G.W.

The Day of Pentecost

———————————•———————————

The Gospel: John 20:19-23

Focus: The Holy Spirit gives each one of us unique talents and abilities so that together we can all help the church run smoothly.

Experience: The children will work together. This will show them that each person has something unique to contribute and that any contribution, no matter how large or small, is important.

Preparation: You will need enough Tinker Toys™ so that each child can have one piece.

Working Together

Today we will see that God has given each one of us certain gifts—special things *we* can do—and that by working together we can do wonderful things we could not do alone. I'm really glad you came up because today I'm going to need a lot of help. We are going to make something that has never been made before. (*Pass out the Tinker Toys™*). Who knows what these are? (*Allow time for responses.*) Right. Tinker Toys™. Now does everyone have the same thing? (*Some will but not all pieces are the same.*) They aren't all the same because we couldn't make anything if everyone had the same pieces. Let's start building, one piece at a time. (*Use child's name.*) Put your Tinker Toy™ here. Who wants to be next? Go ahead and add your Tinker Toy™. (*Continue, allowing all the children to participate, helping them to connect the pieces if necessary, asking what their creation is beginning to look like, complimenting them on a good job. When it's done, continue speaking.*)

This is terrific! (*Hold it up.*) You all worked together and made a wonderful . . . well, what is it? (*There is no wrong answer, so field several, repeating the response and asking if anyone else has an idea.*) Could any one of you have built this with just the one piece you had? Of course not. Each of you used what you had in order to build it together.

That's how it is with doing God's work. God gave each one of us special talents. Each of us can do some things that no one else can do. And God needs each one of us to use our talents and the special things we can do to make the world a better place. When we all work together, doing God's work, we can do great things. **—L.S. and G.W.**

The Holy Trinity—First Sunday after Pentecost

————————————— • —————————————

The Gospel: Matthew 28:16-20

Focus: The use of the word *name* (singular) for the Father, Son, and Holy Spirit shows that the three persons of the Trinity are still only one God.

Experience: Using volunteers from the congregation, the children will explore the names and roles people have. They will see that someone can be more than one "person" even though they have only one name.

Preparation: Choose someone in your congregation who has three rather different roles or positions, for instance, a parent, a singer, and a golfer. Arrange with this person to come forward at the appropriate point in the sermon. Prepare a display surface (newsprint, poster) with the three roles printed on it. On a similar surface print the words *Father, Son,* and *Holy Spirit.* Draw a blank line beside each of the six words so a name can be added.

Three in One

Today we are going to learn about God with the help of some friends in our congregation. Here is a list of three people. Let's read them together. (*Read the three titles: for example, singer, parent, golfer.*) Very good. Now, how many persons are on this list? (*Three.*) That's right.

Now I want us to find out who in our congregation these people are. Whose name can be put by singer? (*They may give several names, including their own. They may need help to find other names from the congregation. But there will be too many names to write.*) Wait! I don't have room for all these names. Let's try the next person on the list. (*Same thing happens.*)

I know what would make our job much easier. Let's try to find one name that we could put for all three persons on this list. What do you think of that? (*Accept all responses.*) Let's see. Is there one person here who is a singer, a parent, and a golfer? (*Have the congregation member come forward and introduce himself or herself. The member explains how he or she is all three people. You should write the one name beside each of the three on the list.*)

Well, we filled up our list because one name fit three different persons. Jesus said the same kind of thing about God in today's Bible verses. He told his disciples to baptize new believers "in the name of the Father and of the Son and of the Holy Spirit" (Matt. 28:19). (*Show second list: Father, Son, Holy Spirit.*) The one name, *God,* fits the three persons of Father, Son, and Holy Spirit. So, what name can we put by each of these three persons? (*God.*) That's right. We worship one God even though we call God by three names: Father, Son, and Holy Spirit. Just like (*give name of congregation member*) is one person who is active in three different ways, so it is with God. Today we celebrate that God is three in one. I hope this will help you understand a little more about what that means. **—C.M.C.**

Second Sunday After Pentecost
—————————————————— • ——————————————————

The Gospel: Matthew 7:21-29

Focus: It is important to listen to the words of Jesus.

Experience: Singing the familiar children's song, "The Wise Man Built His House Upon the Rock" will set the stage for a brief discussion about obeying Jesus.

Preparation: Bring a bag of sand (heavy, clear plastic bag) and a medium-sized rock to show the children. On the bottom of the rock paint "Do what Jesus says." Don't let the children turn the rock over before you are ready for them to see the words.

Building to Last

I'd like us to sing a song today. It is about one person who was wise and one who was foolish. If you know it, sing with me. If you don't know it, you will soon! It goes like this:

> *The foolish man built his house upon the sand* (repeat three times).
> *And the rains came tumbling down.*
> *The rains came down and the floods came up* (repeat three times).
> *And the house on the sand fell flat!*
> *The wise man built his house upon the rock* (repeat three times).
> *And the rains came tumbling down.*
> *The rains came down and the floods came up* (repeat three times).
> *and the house on the rock stood firm!*

Wonderful! Now, which of those two houses would you rather live in: the one on the sand or the one on the rock? (*The one on the rock.*) Me too. Look at this bag of sand. Feel how soft the sand is and how easily it moves. (*You may want the bag open so they can touch the sand itself.*) No wonder a house built on sand would fall down. Now here is a rock. Feel how hard and firm it is. It would make good sense to build a house on a foundation of rock.

It is important for our house to stand firm, but it is even more important for our lives to stand firm. Jesus knows what foundation is best for our lives. Do any of you know what that is? (*Allow time for responses. Encourage ideas such as God, love, Jesus.*)

Let me turn over the rock and you will see a message I put there: "Do what Jesus says." The Gospel for today tells us, "Everyone then who hears these words of mine and acts on them will be like a wise man who built his house on rock" (Matt. 7:24). This is what Jesus tells us. When we do what Jesus says, it shows that we believe in him. In Sunday school and worship and at home you are being taught to do what Jesus says. And Jesus is a good, strong foundation for your life. You can be just like a house built on a rock!

—C.M.C.

Third Sunday after Pentecost
———————————— • ————————————

The Gospel: Matthew 9:9-13

Focus: Jesus came to those in need—those who could not find the "missing piece" of life's puzzle.

Experience: By putting together a puzzle, the children will demonstrate the need for a key piece that holds together all the other pieces. They will learn that God is like that in their lives.

Preparation: Using posterboard or some other large, sturdy material, construct a jigsaw puzzle using the following design:

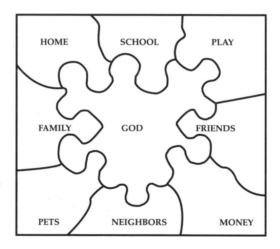

Put the puzzle pieces in a large bag. As the sermon begins, lay out all the pieces except the "God" piece.

Putting Life Together

Children, you may not have noticed it yet, but life can get pretty confusing sometimes. It is hard for people to know what to do. Many people find it hard to put their lives together. Here is a puzzle with pieces that are labeled with many parts of our lives. Let's see if we can put this "life" together. Let's all work together.

(*Allow a minute for them to align the pieces. But the center piece, that holds the others in place is missing, so the puzzle won't hold together well.*)

There is a piece missing isn't there? That makes it hard to put this "life" together. If we had the missing piece, it would hold all the other pieces together so we could live right. What words do you see on these puzzle pieces? (*Help them to read if they are not yet able: home, school, play, friends, money, neighbors, pets, family.*) What piece do you think is missing from our "life" puzzle? (*Affirm their responses. Encourage them to think about ideas like God, Jesus, love.*)

It is the "God" piece! (*Remove this piece from the bag and put it into the puzzle.*) When we put the "God" piece in the center of this puzzle, it holds the others in place. That is what Jesus is trying to tell us about life. He taught us that we need God at the center of our lives in order to keep our lives together.

At times we all have a hard time knowing what we should do. God knows we need help. That is why God wants to be at the center of our lives. And God holds our lives together and helps us. Let's pray and thank God for doing that (*Prayer.*)   **—C.M.C.**

Fourth Sunday after Pentecost

—————————————— • ——————————————

The Gospel: Matthew 9:35—10:8

Focus: Jesus knows our names, and that makes us important.

Experience: This story of a family of children with numbers instead of names can help the children appreciate the love Jesus has for each one individually.

Our Very Own Name

Hi, kids. Let me count you today. (*One, two, three. . . .*) Maybe I should just call you by number instead of by your names. That might be quicker. What would you think about that? (*Allow for both negative and positive responses.*)

I want to tell you a story. Long ago a mother and father had so many children that they did not give them names. Instead they called them by number. "Child number 7, please find child 11." "Child number 4, will you shut the door?" "Child 23, it's your turn to make tea." I told you they had a lot of children! All the other children in the town thought this was very funny. "Why did your parents give you numbers and not names?" they asked. None of the numbered children knew why, so they asked child number 1—who was the first and oldest child—to find out from their parents.

The mother said, "Numbers are easier to remember, child 1."

The father said, "And every number is different."

"But all of us, from 1 to 26, would rather have names like every other child," their son answered.

That night the father saw in his Bible the names of the first twelve disciples of Jesus. As he read them, he thought the names sounded much more interesting than numbers. Peter, James, Andrew, and the rest were much nicer than 1, 2, 3, and so on. *Jesus must think names are important since all 12 disciples' names were listed,* the father thought. Since they did want their children to follow Jesus, the man and his wife decided to give names to their children the very next morning. So when the children came down for breakfast, instead of seeing numbers on their chairs, each child found his or her very own brand-new name! That was the most wonder-

ful breakfast those children ever had. And all 26 of them remem-
bered it for the rest of their lives!

Now, that was just a story, but our names are very
important—to us and to Jesus! Jesus loves each one of us, knows
us by name, and listens when we pray. Let's pray together: Dear
Jesus, we are so glad we each have our own special name. And we
are glad that you love us, you know our name, and you listen
when we talk to you in prayer. We love you too! Thank You.
Amen.   —C.M.C.

Fifth Sunday after Pentecost

———————————— • ————————————

The Gospel: Matthew 10:24-33

Focus: Jesus loves and values each person.

Experience: By counting pennies to buy sparrows, the children will learn how little a bird costs. By comparison, they will learn that human life cannot be bought with pennies. It is very valuable to God.

Preparation: Bring a handful of pennies, enough for each child to have one, and a picture of a sparrow—large enough for all to see.

How Many Pennies?

Good morning! Who knows what a sparrow is? (*A bird.*) Yes, a very small bird. Here is a picture of one (show it). In Jesus' day, sparrows were bought and sold for a very small amount of money. In fact, a person could buy two sparrows for one penny. (*Hold up one penny.*) So, with this penny, how many sparrows could I buy? (*Two*). And if I had one more penny, how many more sparrows could I buy? (*Two more.*) Good! Every penny buys two sparrows.

Here is a penny for each of you. (*Pass out pennies.*) How many sparrows could we buy if we used all these pennies? (*Answer depends on number of children. Accuracy will depend on the age of the children!*)

Now suppose I wanted to buy a child like you. How many pennies do you think that would take? (*A thousand. A million.*)

Well, the fact is, children cannot be bought for money. God gives each of us as a gift to our families. But this is why I'm telling you this story. Jesus said that even the little sparrow that is sold for half a penny is important to God. So if God cares for such little birds, God must care for you *much,* much more! You are very small compared to the big world around you, but each of you is very important to God. I want you to keep the penny as a reminder of how important you are, and how much God cares for you.   **—C.M.C.**

Sixth Sunday after Pentecost
————————————————————————•————————————————————————

The Gospel: Matthew 10:34-42

Focus: God needs to be first in our lives.

Experience: By focusing on their feelings about the people and things they love, children can better understand their relationship to God.

Preparation: Bring something that *you* love: chocolate bar, favorite sweater, picture of a special person to you, or something of this sort.

Loving God

I'm so glad you came up today. We're going to talk about the people and things we love. I brought something I love. (*Briefly describe it.*) What about you? Is there a food you love? (*Allow time for a few responses and allow some discussion.*)

What about television shows? Is there a television show you love? (*Allow time for responses.*)

Do you have pets that you love? (*Responses.*) How about people. Who are the people you love? (*Responses.*)

Can you love all those people and things at the same time? (*Responses.*) Sure you can. Maybe we think love is like a pie, and if we give one piece away and then another, there's less for everyone else. But love isn't like that, it's more like air. Think of how much air there is! So it is with love. We always have enough love to go around.

The more we love other people, the more we know how good love feels. Doesn't it feel good when somebody we know loves us—our mom or dad or grandma or grandpa? Do you love the people who love you? (*Responses.*) Sure you do. Jesus tells us many times how much God loves us. And we know we love God, too, more and more each day.   **—L.S. and G.W.**

Seventh Sunday after Pentecost
———————————————— • ————————————————

The Gospel: Matthew 11:25-30

Focus: Jesus invites us to give him our troubles.

Experience: The children will experience the heaviness of actual weights and the relief of putting them down.

Preparation: Bring a backpack or large purse, and several heavy objects (weights, books, stones).

Giving Jesus Our Troubles

Jesus tells us that we should give our troubles to him, and we will feel a lot better. Today we're going to see how that works.

Who feels strong today and wants to hold this? (*Show the backpack or purse. Choose a volunteer and give him or her the empty pack or purse. Have the child stand.*) Now, (*use child's name*), is this very heavy? (*No, it's not very heavy, yet.*)

Do you ever have a day when nothing seems to go right? (*Allow responses and encourage the children to name a few: falling down, spilling milk, getting into a fight, losing something.*) How do you feel when things like that happen to you? (*Sad, angry. Allow several responses.*)

Let's pretend each one of these (*books, stones*) is something bad that happens. Let's pretend this is (*give one of the responses like falling down*), this is (*give another response*), and this is (*give another*). Is that (*pack/purse*) getting heavy now? Would you like to put it down? (*Allow responses.*) What if I put a few more (*weights*) inside? (*Make it quite heavy.*) All right. You can take it off now. Does anyone else want to try to hold this? (*Allow some children to hold it.*) Would you like to go around all day carrying this heavy bag? (*No.*) You would be really weighted down, wouldn't you?

Well, that's the way it can feel when we have a lot of troubles and worries. They aren't heavy, like the (*weights*), but they can make us feel weighed down. Jesus tells us we can give all these troubles to him. And you know what that is like? Here, I'll show you. (*Stand up and share the weight with the first child so that you are carrying the weight.*) Isn't that better? Jesus helps us carry our troubles. He loves us and will never let us carry them all alone.

When you pray, tell Jesus about your troubles. He is always ready to listen and to help you carry them.

Let's pray together. Thank you, God, for helping us when we have troubles. You know we feel bad when (*mention some of the "bad things" the children named earlier*). It is good to know you are with us, even then, and that you love us always. Thank you, God. Amen.   **—L.S. and G.W.**

Eighth Sunday after Pentecost

———————————————— • ————————————————

The Gospel: Matthew 13:1-9 (18-23)

Focus: No matter what type of "soil" we may be, God still sows his Word among us.

Experience: The sermon will demonstrate the parable of the sower, introducing the idea of growth and change.

Preparation: Bring four flower pots or plastic cups: one filled with rocks, one filled with weeds, one filled with hard-packed dirt, one filled with loose soil. Put them in a low box or a loaf pan.

The Sower and the Seed

Did you know that Jesus tells us people are like soil? We're going to figure out just what he meant.

Suppose you had to plant seeds to grow your own food. What would you want to plant? (*Allow time for responses. You may have to ask leading questions in order to get the children to name vegetables. If the group is only coming up with animals, you could ask what kind of plants you would have to grow to feed them. Or if they suggest cookies, you could talk about planting wheat for flour. Use the names of two kinds of seeds the children have suggested. Then continue.*)

Suppose you had (*name one seed*) seeds and (*another name*) seeds, and you were going to plant them. Which one of these pots would you rather plant them in: (*show the four pots*) this one with the rocks, this one with the weeds, this one with the hard dirt, or this one with the garden soil? (*Ask a specific child.*) Which one would you plant your seeds in? (*Allow time for response.*) Why? (*You may need to steer the responses. It is fine if not every child picks the garden soil. Ask a second and third child as time permits. Then summarize their responses.*)

Today in our Gospel, Jesus tells his disciples that people are like soil, and the things God tells us are like seeds. God speaks to everyone, but some people won't listen. They're like these rocks. (*Show pot with rocks.*) God's Word can't get inside them.

Some don't care. They're like this hard-packed dirt. (*Show it.*) God's Word might get in, but it has a hard time growing.

Some people are too busy. They're like this weedy soil. (*Show it.*) There's no room for God.

Now some people are ready to listen. They care, and they aren't too busy. They hear God's Word, and their faith keeps growing and growing. Which soil are they like? (*The loose soil.*)

God speaks to all of us, no matter whether we are like rocky soil or like rich soil. God keeps on planting seeds in our lives—loving and caring for us. God wants the seeds of faith to grow in each of our lives so that we can experience God's great love for us.

—L.S. and G.W.

Ninth Sunday after Pentecost
————————————————— • —————————————————

The Gospel: Matthew 13:24-30

Focus: God's world is made up of all kinds of people who do all kinds of actions, and we are not to judge them.

Experience: This message will show how labels can be misleading, and that only God can judge what is good or bad.

Preparation: Bring a bowl of grass seed, a bowl of beans or other large seed, and an empty bowl.

What's a Weed?

Today we're going to figure out if we can tell what weeds are. Have you ever seen a weed? What are weeds, anyway? (*Field, repeat, and affirm several answers.*) Basically, weeds are just plants growing some place we don't want them to grow. Who knows what kind of seeds these are? (*Show grass seed.*) Who knows what kind of seeds these are? (*Show beans, then and put them in the empty bowl*). Suppose I plant these beans in my garden and (*add some grass seed*) grass started growing there too. What would be the weed? (*Grass.*)

Suppose I was planting my lawn (add more grass seed to the "mixed" bowl) and beans started growing there too. What would be the weed? (*Beans.*)

Wait a minute. You just told me the grass was the weed. Now you say the beans are weeds? How can that be? (*Children respond.*) Right, whichever one is growing where we don't want it—that's a weed.

So sometimes a plant is a weed, and sometimes it's not. Some grass or bean plants might be good in a certain place but bad in another place. When we label something as good or bad, even plants, we can make mistakes, especially if we don't know the whole story.

The Bible tells us that when we call *people* good or bad, we might also be making a mistake because only God can tell what a person is really like. We are not to judge people. We are not to call a person good or bad. That's a job only God can do. Instead we are to love other people and be good to them because we know God loves them, and God also loves each one of us very much!

—L.S. and G.W.

Tenth Sunday after Pentecost

———————————•———————————

The Gospel: Matthew 13:44-52

Focus: We can look forward to heaven.

Experience: The children will discuss the excitement of finding a hidden treasure and compare that feeling to their expectations of heaven.

Preparation: Bring a shovel, a map, and a Bible.

What Heaven Is Like

Let's pretend we're going to hunt for buried treasure. What is buried treasure, anyway? (*Allow responses.*) Why would someone want to find it? (*Responses.*) Have you ever seen buried treasure? (*Responses.*) Do you think you would want to find it? Why? (*Responses.*)

Well, if we're going to look for buried treasure, what do we need to take with us? (*Show shovel and map when they say them, or add these yourself.*)

Where should we go? (*Suggest a place if no one volunteers one.*) Do you think there still is buried treasure some place in the world? (*Responses.*) It would be fun to find some, wouldn't it?

In today's Gospel Jesus tells us heaven is like buried treasure. We've already figured out what buried treasure is. It's like (*use descriptions of what they told you*). And heaven is like that too. (*Recap responses.*) We've never seen it, but we will have everything we need there.

Do you need a shovel to find heaven? (*No.*) Do you need a map? (*They may say yes or no.*) Well, we *do* have a map, actually a book. We have the Bible (*hold up Bible*). In it Jesus tells us some wonderful things about heaven—everything we need to know. We find out that God has prepared a delightful place for us where we will know God loves us, we will feel happy, and we won't have any more pain or troubles or sadness. Let's thank God for what heaven is like (prayer). **—L.S. and G.W.**

Eleventh Sunday after Pentecost

—•—

The Gospel: Matthew 14:13-21

Focus: No matter how much or how little we may have, God asks us to share what we have with others.

Experience: The children will see that by sharing a little we truly can make a big difference.

Preparation: Bring a large bowl or basket of chocolate chip cookies.

Sharing Makes a Difference

Today we're going to see how sharing a little can make a big difference. Does anyone remember what happened when Jesus collected the five loaves of bread and two fish and tried to feed 5000 people with them? (*Affirm responses and, if necessary, tell the story.*) Were there any leftovers? (*Yes, more than they started with!*)

Suppose I had this cookie (*hold one up*) and I was going to share it with *all* of you. (*Begin breaking off little pieces for each child.*) Would you get very much? (*No.*) No, you really wouldn't get much at all. But if I gave each of you a cookie and asked you to give me back a little piece, let's see what would happen. (*Give each child a cookie and take one yourself.*) I'll start. (*Break off a small piece and put it in the bowl or basket. Then use child's name, if possible, give back a little piece and continue around the entire group until each child has given back a small piece.*)

Wow! Look at all we have! Can you believe how much we got when everyone gave a little? (*Affirm any responses you receive.*)

God asks us to share what we have because God knows that when each of us shares, there will be enough for everybody. So never think you have too little to share. Share what you have, and you can make a big difference for everybody!   **—L.S. and G.W.**

Twelfth Sunday after Pentecost
————————————•————————————

The Gospel: Matthew 14:22-23

Focus: Jesus will help you in times of trouble.

Experience: The children will use life preservers to help them think about safety and faithfulness.

Preparation: Bring two life jackets or other personal flotation devices (PFDs).

Lord, Help Me!

Jesus told his disciples they should hold on tight to their faith in him. Today we'll figure out why.

Let's pretend we're going on a canoe trip. Where should we go? (*Allow responses.*) Fine. Let's go to (*use the place suggested*).

Does a canoe tip over easily? (*Yes.*) Yes, it does. So when you go in a canoe, you should put on one of these. What are these called? Right, life jackets.

I need two volunteers. (*Pick two, one younger and one older child*). When we go in a canoe we should put on a life jacket (*Be putting it on the younger child*). But sometimes people take a life jacket along with them, and they don't put it on. So (*name of a child*), you just sit by your life jacket (*have that child sit on the floor*).

Suppose we are going along (*use a familiar place name*) and suddenly a big wave (*or rapids, if the children have suggested a river*) comes up and your canoe starts rocking and rocking. (*Rock side to side with the children.*) Then the canoe tips over! (*Older child*), your life jacket floats away and you have to swim to shore. You make it, but just barely. (*Younger child*), you had an easier time because you had your life jacket on. Your life jacket helped you to float, so it was easier for you to swim to shore.

Sometimes our life has some scary places. You're going along fine and all of a sudden something goes wrong. That's when we need to remember that Jesus is always with us. He comforts us when we feel sad or worried. And he helps us through our problems. With faith in Jesus, we can be ready for whatever happens.
—L.S. and G.W.

Thirteenth Sunday after Pentecost

————————————————— • —————————————————

The Gospel: Matthew 15:21-28

Focus: Faith is the knowledge and assurance that God will care for us.

Experience: A short story about being lost and then found points out that God watches over us. Faith is trusting in this God who cares for us.

Preparation: Be prepared to tell the story below. (You can change some of the details of the story to fit your own experience.)

Faith

I thought we'd think about faith today. Faith is one of those words that we talk about a lot in church. Let's take a few minutes and try to see what faith is.

Can any of you tell me what faith is? Do you know what we mean by faith? (*Be prepared in case the children can't answer this question. Faith is a difficult concept for children to define. Be ready to answer the question yourself. Say something like, "Faith is trusting in God. It is knowing that God will take care of us and watch over us.*)

Yes, those are good answers. Faith is trusting in God, and it is believing in God. But do you sometimes wonder whether you can really trust God to watch over you and help you? You can, and I'll tell you a story that helps explain why. It's a story that helps me to understand who God is and what it means to have faith in God.

This story is about a boy named John. John was about the age that many of you are. John's family went to visit his grandparents. His grandparents lived on a farm. Their house sat right on the edge of a forest with lots and lots of trees. John's parents told him to be very careful and to not go into the woods because he would get lost.

Well, do you know what John did? (*He went into the woods.*) That's right! John was out playing in the yard. As he played, John decided it would be fun to go into the woods, just a little ways. So John went into the trees and started exploring. He went a little farther and a little farther into the woods. Can you guess what happened? (*He got lost.*)

That's what happened. After John had been walking awhile, he looked around and nothing looked familiar. John got a little worried. He looked for the house, but he couldn't see it. John looked all around, but he didn't know where he was. How do you think he was feeling? (*Scared, lonely, worried.*) Yes, he was very scared. He didn't know where to go or what to do. So John did a very natural thing. He started to cry.

What John didn't know was that his dad had been watching him. When John's dad saw him go into the woods he followed. While John was crying he heard footsteps. He turned around, and sure enough, there was his dad, coming to help him.

Do you think John was happy to see his dad? (*Yes.*) Of course he was! John was overjoyed. His dad could see how scared he was. His dad knew John didn't need to be punished. He gave John a hug then picked him up and took him home.

John learned something that day. The first thing he learned was that when your parents tell you not to do something, you shouldn't do it. But even more important, John learned once again that his dad watched over him and cared for him.

The Bible tells us that God watches over us too. In fact, God watches over us and cares for us even more than our parents. Just like John's dad looked for him and watched over him, God also looks for us and watches over us. Even when we get lost and scared, God promises to be with us.

That means that we can trust in God. We can pray to God and ask for help. And we know that God will watch over us. That's what we mean by faith. Faith is knowing that God loves us very much.

Back on his grandparent's farm, John learned that his dad watched over him. Let's all remember that God our heavenly Father watches over us too. We can live each day with faith in God.

—M.B.

Fourteenth Sunday after Pentecost
———————————————————— • ————————————————————

The Gospel: Matthew 16:13-20

Focus: It is important for us to know who Jesus is.

Experience: Looking at a series of cards that contain statements about Jesus, the children will decide whether they agree or disagree with what is written on each card. In the process you will talk with the children about who Jesus is.

Preparation: Make a series of seven cards. They should be large enough for the children and perhaps the congregation to see. Write one of the following statements on each card:

> *Jesus was born in a hospital.*
> *Jesus is our teacher.*
> *Jesus picked five disciples.*
> *Jesus likes children.*
> *Jesus died and stayed dead.*
> *Jesus is God's Son.*
> *Jesus is our Savior, and he loves us very much.*

Who Is Jesus?

One of the most important questions we can ask is "Who is Jesus?" There is nothing more important than knowing who Jesus is and what he is about. In fact in today's Gospel reading, Jesus asks, "Who do you say that I am?" (Matt. 16:15).

Who is Jesus? Let's talk about that today. I brought along some cards with me. Each of the cards says something about Jesus. Some cards say things that are true, and some say things that are not true. What I'd like to do is show you the cards, one at a time. If you think what it says is true, say yes. If you think it is not true, say no. Now I'll show you the cards, and you say yes or no.

(Show the cards to the children one at a time. Read the cards and discuss each one with the children. Be sure to read the cards because some of the children, and perhaps the congregation, won't be able to read them.)

Here is our first card. *(Hold up and read the first card.)* It says, "Jesus was born in a hospital." Yes or no? *(No.)*

That's right. Jesus wasn't born in a hospital. Where was he

born? (*In a stable, in Bethlehem.*) Very good. He was born in a stable in Bethlehem.

Let's look at the next card. (*Hold up and read the second card.*) It says, "Jesus is our teacher." Yes or no? (*Yes.*) Good. Jesus is our teacher. He teaches us that God loves us and that we are to love God and love others. You folks are good at this!

Let's do another one. (*Hold up and read the third card.*) "Jesus picked five disciples." Yes or no? (*No.*) How many disciples did Jesus have? (*Twelve.*) Of course. Jesus had twelve disciples.

Let's try another. (*Hold up and read the fourth card.*) "Jesus likes children." Yes or no? (*Yes.*) Of course. In fact, the Bible tells us that Jesus *loves* children. He specifically invited children to come to him. Jesus cares for all people, young and old, and everyone in between.

You are really doing well! Here is our next card. (*Hold up and read the fifth card.*) "Jesus died and stayed dead." (*No.*) Very good. Jesus did die. He died on a cross on Calvary. But he rose from the dead. Do you remember what day Jesus came to life again? (*Easter.*) Jesus rose from the dead on Easter, and he still lives today. You really are doing great.

Let's try another one. (*Hold up and read the sixth card.*) "Jesus is the Son of God." (*Yes.*) Yes, of course. In fact today's Gospel reading tells us that Jesus is God's Son.

Let's do one more. This is our last one, and it's really important. (*Hold up and read the seventh card.*) "Jesus is our Savior, and he loves us very much." (*Yes.*) You are so right! Who is Jesus? He is our Savior, and he loves each one of us very, very much. That's the best answer to the question, "Who is Jesus?"

Thank you for your help. You did a great job. You know a lot about Jesus! I'm glad to see that because there is nothing more important than getting to know Jesus. And remember, when we ask the question, "Who is Jesus," the best answer is (*hold up the last card again*), "He is our Savior, and he loves us very much."   **—M.B.**

Fifteenth Sunday after Pentecost

————————————•————————————

The Gospel: Matthew 16:21-26

Focus: To follow Jesus means to do what he does.

Experience: The children will first act out what it means to follow. They will then discuss what it means to follow Jesus.

Following Jesus

I'd like to talk with you today about following, so first let's play a little game. I'm going to ask you to follow me. What that means is that when I do something, you do it. To follow me means that you do what I do. Do you think you can do that? (*Yes.*) Great. Let's give it a try and see if you can follow me.

I'm going to clap my hands. When I clap my hands, you follow by clapping yours. Now I may get a little tricky. I may clap faster or slower. Or I might stop just short of clapping to try to fake you out. Do you think you can follow me? (*Yes.*) Good. Let's go.

(*Clap once and let the children clap. Then start clapping your hands slowly. Be sure the children are following. As the children get into it, try a few different things: clapping your hands up and down instead of side-ways, acting like you will clap your hands but stopping a few inches short to see if the children clap anyway, clapping faster and slower. Have fun with the children, but be sure that the children are following you.*)

You did a great job! You followed me very well. I tried to confuse you a couple of times, but you were too sharp. You did a good job of following me.

In today's Gospel, Jesus tells us to follow him. That means that Jesus wants us to do the same things Jesus did. We follow Jesus by doing things that Jesus did.

Let me ask you a question. What are some things we can do to follow Jesus? Following Jesus means much more than clapping our hands, doesn't it? What are some things we can do to follow Jesus? (*Give the children a chance to answer. Discuss and affirm the answers given. The children will probably say things like, "We can help people," "We can tell people about God," "We can pray." Be sure to affirm the answers.*)

(Also be prepared in case the children don't give any answers. Suggest some answers of your own. Say things like, "Could we follow Jesus by helping people? Of course, that's a good way to follow Jesus." Or "Could we follow Jesus by telling people about God, or by feeding hungry people? Yes, those are all ways we follow our Lord.")

Those are all good answers. Jesus did all those things. He helped people, he told people about God, he prayed, he fed the hungry, he cared for people. We follow Jesus by doing the same things. Jesus calls us to do things like that when he says, "Follow me."

You did a good job of following me when I clapped my hands. That was kind of fun, wasn't it? Let's remember to follow Jesus. There is nothing more important than that. Jesus is our Lord, our Savior. Let's follow him.   **—M.B.**

Sixteenth Sunday after Pentecost

———————————————— • ————————————————

The Gospel: Matthew 18:15-20

Focus: Jesus is with us as we worship.

Experience: The children will learn that Jesus' promise to be present is real for us today. As the children count each other, they will be reminded that Jesus is also in their midst.

Preparation: You will need one large piece of posterboard and a felt-tip marker.

How Many of Us Are There?

I'd like to do a little counting and a little arithmetic with you today. Let's count how many of us are here.

Let's count the girls first. (*Count the girls. Then write the number of girls on the posterboard—seven girls.*) There are seven girls. Now let's count the boys. (*Count the boys. Then write the number of boys under the number of girls.*) So, we have seven girls and six boys. Let's add one pastor. (*Write "one pastor" on the list.*) Now, if you add all that up, there are fifteen people up here. (*Intentionally add one extra to the total. Write that number on the board. Then wait for the children to point out that you added wrong.*)

Some of you are looking at me and shaking your heads. Did I count wrong? Is my adding wrong? Let's count again. (*Count the girls again.*) There are seven girls and there are six boys. (*Count the boys again.*) That makes thirteen. And there is one of me. That makes fourteen. But I wrote down fifteen. Am I wrong? Or is there somebody else here with us? (*Allow time for responses.*)

I believe there is someone else here with us. I believe Jesus is here. In fact, that is Jesus' promise—a promise he makes in today's Gospel reading. Jesus promises that when even two or three people are gathered in his name, he is there too. That means that Jesus is here with us.

That's what makes worship so special. Jesus is here. He is here to listen to us, to help us, to love us.

So, to get back to my addition, there are fifteen of us here. (*Hold up the posterboard again.*) There are seven girls, six boys, one pastor, and Jesus.   —**M.B.**

Seventeenth Sunday after Pentecost
—————————————— • ——————————————

The Gospel: Matthew 18:21-35

Focus: Jesus loves and forgives us.

Experience: The children will talk about forgiveness and learn the sign language words for *Jesus* and *forgiveness*.

Preparation: Be prepared to teach the children two words in sign language. If possible, find someone in the congregation or the community who knows sign language to help you prepare.

The first word will be *Jesus*. Hold your hands in front of you— about eight to twelve inches apart. Indent or bend down the middle fingers of each hand. Bend them down about an inch or so below the other fingers.

Take the middle finger of your right hand and touch the palm of your left. Then take the middle finger of your left hand and touch the palm of your right. That's the sign for Jesus.

The second sign is the sign for *forgiveness*. Hold your left hand out in front of you, with palm up. Your fingers should be together and straightened out. The hand should be flat, parallel to the floor. The fingers should be pointed away.

Slightly cup your right hand with the palm facing downward. Place your right hand above the palm of your left hand with the fingertips of your right hand barely touching the palm of your left.

Starting from a point near the wrist of your left hand, move your right hand straight out over your left hand. The right fingertips should run directly over the ring finger of your left hand.

That's *forgiveness*. It's a bit like pushing something away from you.

Forgiveness

I'd like to teach you some words in sign language today. Does anyone know what sign language is? (*Allow responses.*) Yes, it's speaking with your hands. Some people have trouble hearing, or can't hear at all. Sign language is a way of speaking with your hands so that people who can't hear can still communicate.

I'd like to teach you two words in sign language. The first word is the word for *Jesus*. I like this one. The word for Jesus is like this (*Demonstrate the sign for them. Then encourage them to try it.*)

Why do you think we point to our hands to talk about Jesus? What happened to Jesus' hands? (*They had nails driven in them.*) That's right. Jesus is the one who died on a cross for us. He had nails driven in his hands. The sign for Jesus reminds us of that. Let's make the sign for Jesus again. (*Have the children make the sign.*)

The second sign I'd like to teach you is the sign for *forgiveness*. But before I do that, let's talk about what that means. Does anyone know what the word *forgiveness* means? (*Give the children a chance to answer. They may not be able to answer. Forgiveness is a difficult concept for children to define.*)

Forgiveness is kind of a hard word to describe, isn't it? Let me see if I can explain a bit about it. Do you ever do things that are wrong? (*Responses.*) Sure, we all do. We disobey our parents, or we might take things that don't belong to us, or we hurt people, or we break God's laws. We call these things sin. We all sin. We all do things that are wrong.

What happens when we sin? Things are not good, are they? People become angry with us, and we feel bad. When we do things that are wrong, we get punished. And worse, things just don't go right anymore.

Forgiveness means that our sins are taken away. When we are forgiven, we feel better. Things go right again. It's like being set free! Forgiveness means that our sins are taken away.

Let me show you the sign for forgiveness. It's like this. (*Show and describe the sign for forgiveness to the children.*) Put your right hand over your left and run it across like this. It's like our sins and wrongs are pushed away. It's a neat sign. God takes our sins away from us.

The Bible tells us that because of what Jesus did for us, God forgives us. The good news of Jesus is that he has given his life for us. And because of that, he forgives us all our sins.

So, let's say that, using our signs. Because of Jesus (*make the sign for Jesus*), our sins are forgiven (*make the sign for forgiveness*). Let's say that again. (*Repeat the words and actions.*)

You did great! Thanks for sharing with me. And remember, in Jesus we are forgiven. **—M.B.**

Eighteenth Sunday after Pentecost

—————————————————•—————————————————

The Gospel: Matthew 20:1-16

Focus: The church is a place to welcome all people.

Experience: The children will discuss two signs, one that says, "Welcome" and one that says, "Keep Out." We will then talk about the church being a place that welcomes all people.

Preparation: Bring two signs, one that says, "Welcome" and one that says, "Keep Out." You can buy inexpensive plastic signs at many stores, or you can make the signs with posterboard.

Welcome

I brought two signs with me today. I'd like to show them to you and talk about what they mean.

Here's the first sign. (*Hold up the sign that says, "Welcome."*) (If some children can read, ask this question:) What does it say? (*Welcome.*) That's right. Welcome! What does a sign that says "Welcome" mean? (*It means you are welcome there. You can come in.*) Yes. A welcome sign means, "Come on in." "Everybody come in." "Everyone is invited." A welcome sign means that this place is open to all.

Here is my second sign. (*Hold up the sign that says, "Keep Out."*) (If some children can read, ask this question:) What does this sign say? (*Keep out.*) What does a "Keep Out" sign mean? (*Don't come in. Stay away.*)

That's right. *Keep out* means, "You better not come in here." "We don't want outsiders." "We don't want anybody in here." *Keep out* means stay away.

Suppose we were going to put up one of these signs in our church. (*Hold up both signs.*) Which sign should be put up in here? (*Welcome.*) Of course! The church is a place that welcomes people. We welcome all people. Everybody is invited here. Our church is a place for a welcome sign.

Jesus tells us that. Everyone is invited to his church. It doesn't matter if you are young or old, rich or poor, black or white, Hispanic or Oriental. It doesn't matter if you've been a Christian for sixty years or you are just thinking of becoming a Christian. Jesus, in his love, wants to invite and welcome all people to his church.

Let's leave our welcome sign up here, in the front of the church. (*Place the welcome sign in a place where it can be seen.*) That will help to remind us that the church is a place that welcomes all people.
—**M.B.**

Nineteenth Sunday after Pentecost

————————————————— • —————————————————

The Gospel: Matthew 21:28-32

Focus: We serve and obey God because God loves us.

Experience: The children will sing a song about praising and serving God. They will then talk about why they are to praise and serve God.

Preparation: Plan for the children to sign the song "Praise Him, Praise Him," or another familiar praise song. The children can sign by themselves or with the entire congregation. Ask the organist to accompany you, or arrange for a guitar or piano accompaniment.

Praise God!

I'd like for us to sing a song today. It's a song that many of you know. It's called "Praise Him, Praise Him." The words go like this:

> *Praise him, praise him, all ye little children;*
> *God is love, God is love.*
> *Praise him, praise him, all ye little children;*
> *God is love, God is love.*

Do you think we can sing that? Great. Let's first sing "Praise him, praise him." Then let's do a second verse and sing "Serve him, serve him." Do you think you can remember all that? Good. Let's try it. In fact, let's ask the entire congregation to sing with us. What do you think? Should we ask everyone to sing with us? (*Yes.*) Okay, congregation, please sing along with us! (*Sing two verses— first "Praise him" then "Serve him."*)

I like that song. It reminds us that it is good to praise and serve God. It reminds us to praise God by singing about him and worshiping him. It reminds us to serve God by living our lives as God wants us to live.

Let me ask you a question. We sang about praising and serving God. Why should we do that? Why do we praise and serve God? (*Because God wants us to. Because God loves us. Because God is our Father. Be prepared for a variety of answers.*) Yes. We are God's children, aren't we? God has made us and God loves us very much.

God has claimed us in baptism, and he sent Jesus to be our savior. Because God has done all these things for us, it's good to praise and serve God. In fact, that is something for us to be doing every day of our lives. We are God's children, and there is nothing more important than serving and praising God.

Let's close today by singing one more verse of our song. Let's sing "Love him." As we sing, please remember that we love God because God first loved us. Let's invite the whole congregation to sing with us. (*Close by singing "Love him."*)   —M.B.

Twentieth Sunday after Pentecost

•

The Gospel: Matthew 21:33-43

Focus: Faith is a gift that must be used.

Experience: Children can see through this story what happens when a gift is not appreciated.

Use It or Lose It

This morning I'd like to tell you a story.

Hannah's mother gave her a potted plant on her birthday. At first Hannah liked the plant very much. She put it in the window in her room so it could have sunlight. At first, she watered it two times a week, just the way the instructions told her to.

But Hannah had a lot of other things to do. She had friends. She liked to watch television. She had lots of toys. Sometimes she would forget to water the plant. One day she moved it away from the window into a dark corner. What do you think happened to the plant while it was in the corner with no light and no water? (*Discuss how the plant would wilt, leaves would turn yellow and fall off. Finally the plant would die.*)

One day Hannah's mother saw the poor, sick plant. She took it out of Hannah's room. She cut off the sick leaves and watered the plant. Then she put the plant in Adam's room—Adam is Hannah's older brother. Adam liked the plant and took good care of it. The plant started growing again.

When Hannah saw the healthy plant, she wanted it back. But her mother said no. Hannah did not take care of the plant, so she lost it. It would have died if it had stayed in Hannah's room, so her mother gave the plant to Adam.

Jesus told a story like this. He said God gave a special gift to his chosen people. It was like a vineyard—a place where grapes are growing. But the people didn't remember that God had given them this gift. So Jesus said, "Therefore I tell you, the kingdom of God will be taken away from you and given to a people that produces the fruits of the kingdom" (Matt. 21:43). The people needed to remember that the vineyard was a special gift from God. They should have used the fruit in a way that would honor God. They should have shared it with others.

God has also given us a special gift. He sent Jesus to be our Savior. Jesus shares in our lives. He comes to be with us when we do wrong things, and he forgives us. He is with us to hear our prayers and to help us.

How do you think we can take care of this gift from God? Hannah needed to water the plant and give it sunlight so that it could grow. What can we do to help our faith grow? (*Help the children see that they need to hear the story of Jesus from the Bible, they need to worship him, they need to be with other Christians, they need to serve him.*) All of these things help our faith stay alive and grow.

God has given you the gift of faith. You need to use that faith in a way that honors God. If you have a plant in your house, use it to remind yourself that your faith needs to grow too. Help take care of the plant; and as it grows, give God thanks for the growing plant and thanks for your growing faith.   —E.W.

Twenty-first Sunday after Pentecost
—————————————•—————————————

The Gospel: Matthew 22:1-10 (11-14)

Focus: Evangelism is an invitation to be with Jesus and to invite others to be with him.

Experience: This sermon gives an opportunity for children to experience a simple method of evangelism and to teach it to adults.

Preparation: Examine your method of inviting children to hear the children's sermon. The way we do things easily becomes routine. Here is an opportunity to restate your purpose for these sermons not only for the children and the congregation but for yourself.

Come with Me

Children, I have something I want to say to you, but stay in your seats for just a moment. At this time in our service I usually invite you to come up to hear a special message just for you. I want to remind you why we do this. We have this time because I want to tell you something very important. I want you to hear it in words that you understand and in a way that you know it is meant for you. Now will you come up here for that message? (*Allow some time for the children to come forward.*)

The message I have for you is this: Jesus loves you. He loves you now when you are a child, and he will love you when you are a teenager, an adult, and an old person. In the Bible Jesus tells us the kingdom of heaven is like a big celebration—a party where we are happy together.

We will go to that party when we are in heaven, but Jesus is with us now, so we can also have the party now. Our church service can be like a party. It is a time to be happy and enjoy being with God and each other. That's why I invited you here.

First I invited you to the party. Now you can invite someone else. I want each of you to go back and bring someone else with you to be with us up here. (*Give the children time to bring others up.*)

Now look how many people we have at the party! We have a

message for those that you brought with you. Jesus loves them too, just like he loves you.

Sometimes people won't come to the party when we ask them. Some adults might think that they don't want to be a part of a children's sermon. Many people have other excuses for not coming to be with Jesus. But Jesus doesn't ask us to argue with them. All Jesus asks us to do is invite them.

I hope you adults are happy that these children invited you to come up and share their message with you. All of us can think of our worship service as a party. We are happy because we are together with one another and with Jesus. And all of us can invite others to come to the party with us. **—E.W.**

Twenty-second Sunday after Pentecost

———————————— • ————————————

The Gospel: Matthew 22:15-21

Focus: Thinking about Jesus can help us know how to spend our money.

Experience: Using money is a major responsibility in life. Yet children receive little training on how to use money as a part of their Christian faith. This text offers a great opportunity to help children see not only the need to give to church but also the proper use of money.

Preparation: Bring three one-dollar bills, eight quarters, an offering plate, a child's coin jar, an ad for a toy or book that a child would enjoy, and a sales receipt.

What Do You Do with Money?

Do any of you have any money at home? Do you know what to do with money? (*Talk about spending, giving, and saving. Show the ad to illustrate spending, the coin jar for saving, and the offering plate for giving.*)

We all need to learn how to use our money. Some people tried to trick Jesus by asking if they should pay taxes to a bad government. Jesus showed them some money and said, "Give therefore to the emperor (that is, the government) the things that are the emperor's, and to God the things that are God's" (Matt. 22:21)

That was a good answer. Jesus did not tell them what to do with every dollar they had. Instead he told them to think about their money and to use it in the ways it was needed. Let's do the same thing.

I've got five dollars here, see? Three dollars in bills and two dollars in quarters. Remember the ways that we could use it. You could use some of the money to buy something. (*Show the ad.*) By the way, when you buy something in our country, you are also paying taxes. If you look at your receipt (*show it*), you will see that the store added on some tax. So you use some of your money to buy things you need, and you pay some taxes at the same time.

Also you need to save some money. Maybe you have a jar for

saving money. (*Show them the coin jar.*) I hope some of you have a savings account at the bank.

And you need to give some of your money to others. You can give money to the church. The money is used to teach others about Jesus, to help people who have problems, and to help us all work together. The church uses the money to do the things Jesus wants us to do.

Notice that I haven't told you how you have to divide your money. If you had five dollars, how would you divide it? (*Let the children talk about different ways of dividing the money and other ways of using it. This part of the discussion could get too complex for very young children. You might want to put all the money in the coin jar for now and decide later how to use it.*)

Remember, Jesus didn't say that you should give all of the money to the church. But you can use all of your money in a Christian way. Because Jesus is our Savior, we get to do church things. We worship, go to Sunday school, and do other things here. But Jesus is with us in *all* parts of our lives. He is with you at home, at school, and when you are with your friends.

One way to remember that Jesus is a part of all of your life is to remind yourself that all of your money is a gift from him. You can spend it, save it, and give it as a way of being thankful to him.

—E.W.

Twenty-third Sunday after Pentecost
——————————————— • ———————————————

The Gospel: Matthew 22:34-40

Focus: Many people see Christianity as only a moral system—laws to tell them how to live. Jesus says love is the most important thing.

Experience: This sermon gives the children an opportunity to experience lots of laws, or one way of love.

Preparation: Bring two large sheets of paper or posterboard and a marker.

Love Is the Way to Go

Let's pretend that your family is talking about getting a dog. You want the dog, but your parents think that you might not take care of it. So the family decides to make a list of the things that you would have to do if you have a dog. Let's make the list now. (*List all the things the children suggest as rules they must have to own a dog. As fast as possible, get them past the easy ones: feed, water, bathe, walk, clean up mess. Then include: medical attention, provide toys, pay for licenses, provide for care while family is away, and so on.*)

Do you think that this list is complete? Maybe after you had the dog you would find that there are other things you would have to do—things you didn't think about. Look at how long the list is, and there will be more later!

Now let's make another list. (*On the second sheet of paper write "Love the Dog."*) Look at all the rules on the first list. The second list says only one thing. But if you loved the dog, would you feed it? (*Quickly go through the first list and show that if you loved the dog, you would do all of those things.*)

We also need rules to live with people. We have many rules that tell us how to live with others. A man once asked Jesus which rule was the most important. Jesus said, " 'You shall love the Lord your God with all your heart, and with all your soul, and with all your mind.' This is the greatest and first commandment. And a second is like it: 'You shall love your neighbor as yourself.' On these two commandments hang all the law and the prophets" (Matt. 22:37-40).

Jesus tells us to do two things. Love god and love people. We can love God because God loved us first. God sent Jesus to be our Savior. Jesus loved us so much that he gave his life for us. Jesus loves all people so he tells us to love everyone that he loves.

We need rules when we forget that God loves us and we can love one another. But rules don't always help us. We don't always do what the rules tell us to do. That's why we need Jesus. He loves us even when we do things that are wrong. He gives us love so we can love others—even when they are wrong.

Remember this one word (*point to "love"*), not as a rule, but as a way to live. It is the way God has blessed you. And it is the way you can enjoy being with God and others.   **—E.W.**

Twenty-fourth Sunday after Pentecost
———————————————— • ————————————————

The Gospel: Matthew 25:1-13

Focus: The joy of the gospel can encourage an active faith.

Experience: The children will see two examples of responding to a message.

Preparation: Print the messages below and put them in two envelopes.

Are You Ready?

Does your mother or father ever leave a message for you when you come home from school? (*Ask where they leave the message. Do they write it? Do they leave messages for the baby-sitter or day-care provider? Do they have an answering machine on the phone?*)

I have two messages, each in an envelope. Let's pretend they are on the refrigerator door. Why do parents often put messages on the refrigerator door? (*Let children respond.*) This envelope is for (*give to a child from the group*). And the second one is for (*give to another child from the group.*) Will you two please come up and look at the messages? (*We will use the names Brandon and Kelsey. You use actual names of children in your group.*)

Brandon, you see your name on the envelope. You think you know what the message will be. Your mother will tell you to clean your room, do your homework, and eat an apple. Your mother always says things like that. So, you pretend you don't see it and go watch television. Brandon, sit over there. (*Indicate area off to the side.*)

Kelsey, you also see your name. You open the envelope (*let child open it*) and it says, (*you or child can read the message*) "Hurry up and do your chores and homework because tonight I want to take you out for hamburgers, and we will go shopping." Kelsey hurries and gets her work done. (*Kelsey can mime doing chores off to the other side.*)

When their mother comes home, she says, "Are both of you ready?" Brandon is still watching TV. Kelsey has all her chores done. So their mother arranges for a neighbor to stay with Brandon while she and Kelsey go out for hamburgers and shopping. The message for both children was the same. (*Open the other envelope and read the message.*) But Brandon didn't read it.

Jesus tells a story about some women going to a party. Some were like Brandon. They didn't listen to the message and get ready. Some were like Kelsey. They listened and were ready for the party. Jesus said he would come back again, "Keep awake therefore," he said, "for you know neither the day nor the hour" (Matt. 25:13). (*Have the two children rejoin the group and thank them for being good actors.*)

God has a message for us. It is in the Bible. Some are like Brandon pretended to be. they think they know all about God, so they don't bother to read the Bible or listen to it, or learn about it.

But others are like Kelsey pretended to be. They read the Bible and learn about it and find that God loves them. God has given his Son to be their Savior. He wants to be with them at all times. He wants them to be ready to come to his party in heaven.

I'm glad that you are here today to listen to God's message. Always remember that God has something to say to you because God loves you. Read the Bible. Listen to your teachers. Learn about God. When Jesus asks if you are ready, I want you to be able to say yes. **—E.W.**

Twenty-fifth Sunday after Pentecost
———————————————•———————————————

The Gospel: Matthew 25:14-30

Focus: Dreams can become plans that really work.

Experience: The children will listen to a story and talk about their own dreams and plans.

You Don't Start at the Top

How many of you have a dream—something you hope might happen? Can you tell me what some of your dreams are? (*Allow time for responses. You may need to prompt them by asking questions like, "Do you dream of becoming a firefighter or an Olympic athlete or of going to Disneyland or of being rich?"*) It's fun to share our dreams with others. Dreams are important. They give us something to hope for and plan for and work toward.

Today I'm going to tell you a story about a boy named Jason, who had a dream. Jason felt excited. His fourth-grade class planned to perform a musical play. The lead part called for a boy who could sing and dance. Jason had already been singing in the school choir. He had also taken some dance lessons. He knew he could get the part.

But Jason grew so excited about being in the play that he forgot everything else. He dreamed about what it would be like to be on stage. His parents and grandparents would come to see him. Maybe his picture would be in the paper. Then maybe the television news would show him singing and dancing.

Jason dreamed about what it would be like if someone from Hollywood saw him on television. A director would call him, and Jason would get a part on a television program—then maybe a movie. Jason forgot about his friends. He forgot about his school work. He could only dream about being a star!

You have daydreams about what you want to be when you grow up. So did Jason. Most people do. It's fun to think about being famous or rich. It's ok to have daydreams. But listen to the rest of the story about Jason. He made a mistake that I hope you won't make.

When the teacher announced who got to be in the play, Jason's name wasn't on the list. He didn't get the lead part. He didn't get to be in the play at all. He asked the teacher why. The teacher showed Jason his grades. He had been so busy daydreaming about being a television star that he had not listened in class. He had not done his homework. The teacher said that if he could not get good grades in his school work, he could not be in the play.

Jesus has a message for people like Jason—and for us too. He told a man who did a small job the right way, "Well done, good and trustworthy slave; you have been trustworthy in a few things, I will put you in charge of many things; enter into the joy of your master" (Matt. 25:23).

Jesus tells us that we need to learn how to do little jobs well. Then we will be ready to do more important things. Jesus not only said that—he did it. When he lived on earth, he did many things that didn't seem big and important. He washed his disciples' feet. He helped people no one else liked. He spent time with women and children at a time when most people ignored them. After he had done the small jobs, he did a very important thing. He became our Savior by dying for us and by coming back to life so we can live with him forever.

It seems like a small job to be kind to your friends or your brothers and sisters, but it's important. It seems like a small job to do your homework, but it's important. It seems like a small thing to go to Sunday school, but it's important. Jesus wants us to learn to do the small things well; then we'll be ready for bigger things. —**E.W.**

Twenty-sixth Sunday after Pentecost

•

The Gospel: Matthew 23:1-12

Focus: Self-esteem can reflect biblical truths.

Experience: The children will have a chance to tell about things they can do well and will learn that they can be proud of their abilities.

I Did Great!

This is a story about two sisters, Beth and Judy. The story starts on the day before they got their first report cards of the year. The girls' father asked what kind of grades they thought that they would get.

"I did great!" Beth said. "I will get straight A's. My teacher likes me, and I have lots of friends. I almost never have to study because I'm so smart."

Judy frowned and said, "I didn't understand some of the questions on my social studies test, so I might not get a good grade there. I worked hard in math, but I don't understand fractions very well. I hope I will have at least C's"

The next evening the sisters brought home their report cards. Judy was very happy. She said "I did great!" But Beth was very sad. She said, "This is horrible!" Their parents looked at the report cards. Both girls had mostly B's. Their grades were the same, but Beth felt sad and embarrassed because she had bragged that she would have straight A's even though she hadn't worked very hard. But Judy felt excited and happy. She had expected C's, and she knew she wasn't perfect.

Jesus tells us, "All who exalt themselves will be humbled, and all who humble themselves will be exalted" (Matt. 23:12). If we try to make ourselves look great, we will make ourselves look bad. However, if we are honest about who we are, we can feel good about ourselves.

All of us have talents. We can do some things very well, and it's right to be proud of ourselves. God has given us those talents and we should use them. But when we talk only about how great we are, then our pride becomes bragging, and we can end up thinking we're better at something than we really are. Does that mean we should think that we are no good at all? (*No.*) No way! But we can be honest and tell the truth about ourselves. And we can try to do the best we can. What are some things you do well? (*Accept children's responses.*)

Jesus taught us this lesson to help us know ourselves. He knows us, and he knows we need help. He is our friend, and that's why he promises to be with us and to hear our prayers. That's why he is our Savior. When we know Jesus loves us, we know that we are very special. We can trust him to take care of us, and we can be truly happy with ourselves. **—E.W.**

Twenty-seventh Sunday after Pentecost
—————————————————— • ——————————————————

The Gospel: Matthew 24:1-14

Focus: The Bible tells us what we need to know about Jesus.

Experience: The children will have a chance to compare something real to something artificial. They will also have a chance to share what they already know about Jesus.

Preparation: Bring an artificial banana and a real banana (or some other type of fruit).

Don't Be Fooled

Do you know what this is? (Show the artificial banana.) How do you know? (*Allow responses.*) What do we do with bananas? (*After they talk about eating bananas, offer it to the children to eat. Then talk about why they can't eat it.*) Is it really a banana? (*No, it only looks like a banana.*)

What is this? (*Show the real fruit.*) How is it like the other one? (*Same color, shape, size.*) How is it different? (*One is real; one is not.*) If you are only going to look at them, you can say both of these are bananas. But if you are going to eat a banana, you had better find out which one is real.

Now let's talk about Jesus. Is he real like this (*show the real banana*), or is he pretend like this (*show the other*)? (*He is real.*) Tell me some of the things you know about Jesus. How do you know he is real? (*He was born. He had family and friends. He did things like we do. He died. He rose.*)

Jesus is real. But he warned us to watch for people who would pretend to be like him. He said, "Beware that no one leads you astray. For many will come in my name, saying, 'I am the Messiah!' and they will lead many astray" (Matt. 24:4-5).

When Jesus says, "beware," he is telling us to watch out—to be careful. He says, "Don't be fooled!" Sometimes people will tell you false things about Jesus. You need to know the real Jesus if you are going to believe in him, just as you need to know the real banana if you are going to eat it.

Some people may tell you that Jesus won't love you unless you are good. But that's not true. Jesus loves us even when we do wrong things. That's why he came to be our Savior. He helps us when we do wrong things by forgiving us and by helping us do good.

Some people may tell you that Jesus will come on Judgment Day next week or next month. But Jesus tells us that we don't know when that day will come.

We want you to know the Bible so you can find out about Jesus there. You need to know who the real Jesus is. How can you learn about the real Jesus? (*Worship, Sunday school, parents, the Bible, Bible camp, prayer, church activities.*) All of these things can help you get to know the real Jesus. But always remember the most important thing about Jesus: Jesus loves you.   **—E.W.**

Christ the King—Last Sunday after Pentecost

———————————————— • ————————————————

The Gospel: Matthew 25:31-46

Focus: Christ is king of all.

Experience: The children will be encouraged to imagine how acts of kindness toward someone can make everyone feel happy.

Who Gets the Gift?

Jesus tells us a strange story in today's Gospel. At first it sounds like he made a mistake. He thanks people for feeding him, but they hadn't given him anything to eat. He thanks people for giving him a drink, but they hadn't done it. He thanks them for giving him clothes and for visiting him in prison, but they didn't do those things. Did Jesus make a mistake? Did he give the thanks to the wrong people?

No. Jesus knew what he was talking about. He explained it when he said, "Truly I tell you, just as you did it to one of the least of these who are members of my family, you did it to me" (Matt. 25:40). Jesus says that if people helped those whom he loved, it was the same as if they had helped him.

What is the best gift you ever received? (*Allow responses.*) How did you feel when you received it? (*Responses.*) Suppose your father and mother have a friend that you don't even know. That friend likes your parents and wants to give them a gift. He can't think of anything to give *them,* so he gives *you* a gift—maybe a (*suggest a few gifts they mentioned*). Would that make you happy? (*Sure it would.*) Would it make your parents happy? (*Sure it would.*) Your parents love you. When people give you a gift, they feel as though they got the gift too. It makes them happy to see that you are happy. Who got the gift? (*You did.*) Yes. You did, but your parents did too.

Parents feel that way about their children, and Jesus feels that way about everyone. If you help someone who is hurt, Jesus feels that you have helped him. He feels good if you help someone feel good, because he loves us all.   **—E.W.**